MW00945189

The Day Tripper

By: Len Berman

*Robert,
I hope
you enjoy
the read.
Len*

ISBN:1981689834

ISBN:9781981689835

DEDICATION

I dedicate this book to my lifelong friends;
Kris, Norm, Bob, and Perry.

Torque Masters Forever

Cover art: Mixed media by Len Berman

SPECIAL THANKS

I would like to thank my former wife and close friend, Joellen McQuaid for her help and guidance while writing this book. Joey kept my story on point and provided me with encouragement and direction.

I'd also like to include Linda Payne Smith and her students at the Grossmont Creative Writing Class. Their advice, editing, and friendship will not be forgotten. I couldn't have written this without them.

Thank you - Len Berman

A WHOOSH OF WATER RUSHED PAST AS THE WEIGHT OF THE SUNKEN HULL TRAPPED MY LEGS IN THE MUCKY MARINA BOTTOM. *THE BUOYANCY DRUM MUST HAVE COME LOOSE! SHIT, FUCK! FUCK!!*

CHAPTERS

1	A SIXTEEN FOOT SPEEDBOAT	9
2	OUR MAIDEN VOYAGE	25
3	GORDON PARK	31
4	CEDAR POINT	43
5	STASH	57
6	55TH STREET MARINA	61
7	THE GLENVILLE RIOTS	69
8	RAT FISHING	73
9	OUR NEW BOW RAIL	77
10	NAVIGATING	81
11	HENRY'S BAD DAY	89
12	THE COMMANDO RAID	95
13	THE BIG PARTY	101
14	THE ROAD TO MIAMI	109
15	THE TROPICS	123
16	OUR SECOND YEAR	143
17	MEMORIAL DAY	155
18	CANADA	161
19	FIREWORKS DERECHO	167
20	THREE COP CARS	183
21	THE RICHARDSON	189
22	THE BEGINNING OF THE END	207
23	THE END OF THE END	219
	EPILOGUE	227

CHAPTER 1:
A SIXTEEN-FOOT SPEEDBOAT

In early February of 1968 Kris, Norm, and I drove east on Lake Shore Boulevard in my blue Camaro. We were on our way to check-out a sixteen-foot water-ski boat listed in the classifieds for $1,500. The boat dealership was located twenty miles east of town, along the mouth of the then-frozen Chagrin River. We didn't have anywhere near that kind of money, but if we liked the boat I was confident we could make some kind of a deal.

Little did we know that events over the next hour would impact our lives forever.

* * *

My story begins in 1960. Kris, Norm and I met our first year at Roosevelt Junior High School in Cleveland Heights, Ohio. My name is Lenny Berman.

Kris and I were in the same homeroom and Norm shared a couple of my classes, but we didn't yet know each other. It wasn't until the following winter that we actually spoke.

I was outside my house on East Overlook Road shoveling the sidewalk after a fresh snowfall. I noticed two guys in the street, carrying shovels and coming my way. As they got closer, I recognized them from school and said, "Hey, aren't you in my homeroom?"

"Yeah—I'm Kris."

And so it began. They helped me shovel my sidewalk that day, and we've been fast friends ever since. We were a three-man shoveling crew in the winter, and lawn cutters and leaf rakers the rest of the year. We always found ways to make extra cash.

Kris, Norm, and I hit it off right from the start. Back then, I was building a mini-bike in my basement and the guys helped me finish it. We soon developed a bond that included mechanical stuff, fireworks, BB guns, and girls.

The mini-bike was a bad design, it only ran once, traveling about twenty-feet under it's own power before it broke. Our next project was a full-size motorbike.

Norm Pearlman and I were from Jewish families although neither of us was religious. Friends would describe us as class clown types and we certainly fit the bill. Kris Wilson, from a military family, was more disciplined. He and his siblings always addressed their parents as *Sir* and *Ma'am*, and neither parent had to make a request twice. I wasn't used to that kind of formality, but I got along well with his mother; his father was on deployment most of the time.

Kris, blonde, confident, and good-looking knew how to schmooze the girls. He balanced out our small group and many times became the voice of reason.

By the middle of winter, the motorbike was done. We built it from Kris' old Schwinn frame and the engine from the former mini-bike. The gas tank and throttle came from an old *Whizzer* motorbike. Below is the only picture of our creation.

In the photo, Kris is on the left, next to him, Norm, and then me with the pompadour haircut. On the far right is Scott, Kris' older brother.

The big drive-belt pulley on the rear wheel was the final part to arrive. It came in the mail that afternoon and I immediately installed it. The bike looked good and we were ready to try it out.

Twenty minutes later, we all met at Kris' house for the first ride. As luck would have it, Kris' mom had a new roll of film and took the picture. Scott jumped into the frame at the last second.

After finding out we were taking the bike to the high school parking lot, Scott invited himself along.

Nearby, Cleveland Heights High School's teachers lot was the size of a football field. Mostly empty on weekends, there was plenty of space to try out our motorbike. A recent snowfall had been plowed and traffic patterns around the lot were clear. A tall chain-link fence surrounded the lot. The gates were seldom locked.

Once there, Scott bullied his way into taking the first ride insisting it was for our safety.

"I'll be your test pilot," he said. "One of you could get hurt."

The motorbike ran well as Scott took a few laps around the lot at a low speed. Then he twisted open the throttle to full power to see how fast the bike would go.

I stood at center-lot as Scott sped by yelling something I couldn't understand. He continued to accelerate moving too fast to make the upcoming turn.

I watched in disbelief as he plowed straight into the chain-link fence at full speed. Scott hit so hard that the wire fabric tore loose from the fence posts stopping the motorbike in about five-feet. We always referred to this as a real-life Wile E. Coyote moment.

Scott smashed his nuts big-time. He ended up with a black eye and lots of scrapes and bruises. The motorbike never ran again.

When Scott gave it full throttle, the twist-grip had jammed wide open. All he could do was hold on and brace for impact. Scott never offered his test pilot services again.

* * *

Six Years Later...

The boat dealership occupied a large cinder-block building just off the north side of the road. Through a large display window, you could see that the place was busy, even in the middle of winter. Once inside, we met John, the owner, who looked to be in his mid-thirties. He offered to drive us down to the river valley to have a look at the ski-boat.

Climbing into his van, we headed down the hill to the boatyard below. Hundreds of boats were stored for the winter, lined up in neat rows along the winding frozen river. John located the speedboat and dropped us off.

While exiting his van, I asked him about a large white boat that seemed out of place in a wooded area that we passed along the road. I pointed it out to Kris and Norm as we drove by. The boat, surrounded by trees, sat about a hundred yards away.

John said "That piece of shit! I'd sell it for fifty dollars, just to finally get it out of my boatyard!"

He drove off, saying "Come up to the office when you're finished looking at the boat."

"Fifty dollars," I said to my friends. "That's right in our price range."

Kris and Norm practically read my mind. "Let's go check it out."

We didn't give the ski-boat another thought, never even lifted the tarp. Kris and Norm followed me over the big boat to have an up-close look. As we got closer, the boat looked bigger and the possibilities began to rush through my mind.

The boat half-hidden in the woods, might not have even been visible in summer when the trees were covered by leaves. With so many small trees surrounding it, the boat must have been there for years. Its riveted steel hull at first looked balanced on its keel, but getting closer I saw three wood braces holding it upright. The boat was pointed on each end like a big lifeboat, and in fact, that's exactly what it once was.

A bronze plate attached to the steel hull said it was thirty-five feet in length with a beam of twelve feet. This boat had the "bones" of a real party boat. I liked it already.

Without a tarp to protect it, the weather had done its damage. But at fifty dollars for the boat, we could afford to put some money into repairs.

I turned to see Norm and Kris with smiles on their faces and the same glimmer in their eyes. I think they saw what I saw. In that moment, I knew this vessel and our nautical aspirations harmoniously connected.

Under the hull, an old rickety ladder lay on the ground. I grabbed it, propped it against the gunwale, and climbed up. My first view from atop the ladder left a lasting impression. For an instant, I imagined myself standing at the wheel, wind blowing through my hair and a sea-breeze in my face. I had yet to set a foot onboard, but I was already sold on the boat.

I paused, smiled, and stepped onto the rear deck. It was large, around twelve by twelve-foot, tapering to a point at the stern.

In the middle of the rear deck a five-foot wide hatch opened to a compartment where a remarkably clean flathead six-cylinder engine was mounted on a solid inner frame of thick treated hardwood beams.

Forward of the deck, a weathered, warped padlocked door led to the main cabin. I jimmied the rusted hasp and went inside. The cabin measured fourteen-feet long and twelve-feet wide. A scent of old mildew and dust was in the air. The room was unfinished, but it looked like a good Spartan design. The main cabin slept two on a convertible dinette and a third person on a large couch. The half-finished upholstery on the dinette seats looked like a job abruptly stopped. Rusted tools sat in place covered with dust, they waited to complete the job they had started. I wondered what happened, why was the restoration work stopped in mid-job.

I stepped into the separate forward cabin and saw two large V-berths with storage beneath and an anchor locker under the bow. The main cabin had a propane gas stove, a refrigerator, small galley sink, and an unfinished bathroom that needed a marine toilet.

Everything required attention, but it was easy to visualize how the boat would look when restored. The main cabin was spacious and Kris, at six-foot-three, could stand without hitting his head.

Without a winter tarp to protect it, the deck looked warped in many places. After spending an hour checking things out, we determined that the boat needed interior finishing work and probably a new deck. The riveted hull, made of galvanized steel, seemed to be in good shape with the exception of a fist-sized gash near the bow that looked like an easy repair. A boatyard vehicle may have bumped the hull causing the hole.

We couldn't check the engine and gearbox, but agreed to take a chance on the mechanical stuff.

Somehow, it seemed luck was with us, the planets aligned, and unseen forces guided us to this place, on this very day. A once-in-a-lifetime offer presented itself to us; a fricken' cabin cruiser for fifty dollars. I hoped John was serious about the price.

The temperature dropped with the daylight and the numbing cold couldn't be ignored any longer, but we agreed, we wanted to buy the boat. Walking up the hill to the office we checked our wallets. I had six dollars, Norm five, and Kris had seven. We wondered if John would really sell us the boat for fifty dollars. I wasn't going to give him the opportunity to back out. We planned to approach him as though the sale was a foregone conclusion.

In the office, I shook John's hand as I handed him the folded wad of eighteen dollar and said, "We'll take the fifty dollar boat."

John's hand froze mid-handshake for what seemed like a long moment. Then he said, "Congratulations boys, you bought yourself a boat."

John told us he wasn't sure if the motor ran. If it didn't, we'd have to buy a replacement from him. He also said he'd launch the boat, come spring, for no additional charge. As the three of us left that showroom, we had to be the happiest three souls on the planet.

Driving home, we discussed names for the boat when the song *"Day Tripper"* by the Beatles played on the radio. We looked at each other, shook our heads in agreement, and just like that our boat had a name.

The following week after paying John the thirty-two-dollar balance, we owned the big boat free and clear. We were yachtsmen!

John told us the previous owner died years ago and the original title wasn't in his possession. He would have his lawyer get a new one issued by the county courts after filing a lien for his storage fees. He'd have the title for us in a week or two.

* * *

When the weather got better, Kris borrowed a chainsaw and cut down the trees between the boat and the road, clearing a path through the woods to facilitate repairs.

The boat was built in 1941 by The Welin Davit Company of Perth Amboy, New Jersey. Originally it was a pre-World War II era double-ended lifeboat, probably for a Victory Ship or a freighter.

The once lifeboat, eventually sold as salvage and somehow made its way into John's boatyard in the early sixties. We heard an older gentleman bought the hull and converted it into a cabin cruiser. But he died before completing the job, and the unfinished boat sat for five years, as trees sprouted and grew, around it.

The deck, warped by exposure, needed replacing, but that would come later. Right now the engine had to run and the hull required sanding, primer and paint. At that point our focus was a seaworthy hull.

I went to work on the engine and Kris and Norm started on the hull. After hooking up a jumper from my car battery, which was now on the deck beside me. I hit the start button, the starter motor hummed loud as if trying to turn, but nothing happened.

The engine would not crank over. Even with the help of a large four-foot breaker bar for leverage, we couldn't budge the flywheel. A replacement engine from John would cost almost a thousand dollars, and we didn't have that kind of money.

I had an idea that I thought might un-seize the engine. I removed the spark plugs and squirted oil into each cylinder. Then, I placed our three car batteries side-by-side on the deck beside the engine hatch. Using a few jumper cables, I connected our three car batteries in series. I jury-rigged a high powered thirty-six-volt battery with a shitload of cold cranking amps. That much voltage, I surmised, should produce enough starter motor torque to forcefully spin the flywheel.

To pre-test my concept, I planned to engage the starter button for one quick blip, to see what happens. What happened sure surprised the hell out of me! When I tapped the starter button all hell broke loose as the solenoid relay contacts welded themselves together! The high powered current destroyed everything from the batteries to the starter motor during the four-second calamity.

Sparks flew, wires melted, and smoke poured out of everywhere! I watched the inside of the starter motor glow bright red before everything burned-up. A strong electrical smell of fried ions and burnt insulation permeated the air.

As if things weren't bad enough, our three car batteries were destroyed, it was getting dark and we were alone in the river valley. My bad.

That night we slept aboard the *Day Tripper* for the first time. Kris and Norm, although good sports about it at the time, still tease me to this day about that blunder.

***

Our big concern—the engine might need replacing. If so, where would the money come from? Also, the ice on the river had melted and we had a deadline looming. The boat had to be out of the yard by the end of the month, only three weeks away.

I called our good friend Bob Swan, a talented mechanic, who told me to let him know if we ever needed any help. I could tune an engine, but Bob could take one apart and put it back together. We needed help.

I first met Bob when we were five years old, my family moved from the inner-city to a house in the suburbs a few doors down from Bob. He was my first friend in Cleveland Heights.

He suggested we fill each cylinder and the

crankcase with a product called *Marvel Mystery Oil*, a special type of penetrating lubricant that needs to sit in place for a full week to do its mystifying work. Bob had used the *mystery oil* before to successfully revive an old seized motorcycle engine.

I followed his advice, and after waiting the full week, I attached a breaker bar to the flywheel and the three of us each found a handhold.

I counted "One, two, three, go!"

We tugged at that bar with all our might, after resisting for a moment, the flywheel began to turn. We'd done it! Oil squirted from the empty spark plug holes as we continued to rotate the flywheel.

Norm's dad rebuilt the starter motor at his transmission shop. Bob and I installed it along with a new solenoid, voltage regulator, and all the wiring. We drained and exchanged the *mystery oil* for fresh motor oil, changed the spark plugs, set the timing and we were ready to give it another try.

If the old *Grey Marine* engine didn't start, we were screwed. I crossed my fingers, looked skyward for Divine cooperation, and pushed the starter button.

The engine cranked and cranked, then it fired, backfired and stalled! On the next try, it coughed, popped and fired a few more times, sputtered, smoked and backfired again. I made some adjustments and the engine ran rough for a few seconds, but we failed to coax it fully to life. Soon with the engine flooded, we gave up for the day. Kris took the boat battery home to re-charge it.

The next morning, I got to the boat early. Kris arrived before me and finished installing the re-charged battery. As I came up the ladder to the rear deck, Kris climbed out of the engine hatch went to the console to press the starter button. The engine cranked over a few times then it started and stayed running, shaky as hell at first, but it continued running!

We both yelled a resounding "Yesssss!"

I high-fived Kris and we danced around the rear deck like a couple of giddy school girls.

Without a water supply to cool the motor, we could only run it fifteen minutes at a time. Then after a thirty-minute break to cool the block down, we'd start it again.

We repeated that routine the rest of the day, tweaking the timing and carburetor settings, as needed. At first, it blew a lot of smoke but by dark, the engine burned clean, started quickly and ran smooth. We let John know we were ready to *put-in*.

About that time, we learned a little more about the *Day Tripper's* past. A local resident, who'd heard we were working on the boat, paid us a visit to share some information. He told us six or seven years earlier he happened to be in John's boatyard when the lifeboat hull arrived. He befriended the old man who converted it into a cabin cruiser.

The original owner, a retired carpenter in his seventies, had purchased the lifeboat from an auction in Buffalo. He had it towed by water, to John's boatyard. The carpenter worked on the conversion over that entire summer, planning to launch the boat the following year.

The local man told us that he returned again the following spring to check on the boat's progress. At that time he helped the old man remove the winter tarp. The conversion was nearly completed; only painting and upholstery work remained. The engine ran and the old man said that the boat would launch within a month.

The following year, on his next visit to John's boatyard, he was surprised to see the big boat still sitting in the same spot. Sadly, he found out that the old man became ill and passed away.

I thanked him for bringing us up to date on the boat's origin. He was glad to see that the boat would actually be enjoyed by someone.

CHAPTER 2:
OUR MAIDEN VOYAGE

With the boatyard work done, the rest of the restoration would take place at our new slip, where we'd have electrical power. We'd made arrangements for summer dockage at Gordon Park Marina, near downtown Cleveland.

The night before launching, Kris brought a date to the boatyard and in the dark, quiet river valley, he was the first of us to score aboard the *Day Tripper*. Kris told us about the deed as we drank early morning coffee waiting for the arrival of John, and his *Travelift* boat crane.

As a christening ritual, we had bought a bottle of champagne that we planned to shake-up and spray all over us and the bow. However, while walking behind the boat/crane combo, Kris let us know that he and his date had already drank the champagne. So we decided that Kris' romantic adventure, hours earlier, had been a more suitable christening after all. At least the champagne was put to good use.

I was surprised to see a small crowd at the pier waiting for our launch. Over the years the big white boat had gained notoriety in the boatyard due to its seclusion and haunting look, half hidden by the trees.

As the *Day Tripper* was lowered into the water, I waited for the crane-slings to go slack then I jumped aboard. Looking into the open engine hatch I was shocked to see water pouring in from the through-the-hull fitting around the prop-shaft. I frantically waved my arms to signal John to take it back up.

The leaking fitting, we found out, is called the stuffing box. It's the waterproof bushing that supports and lubricates the turning propeller shaft.

Fortunately, a couple veteran boaters who witnessed our predicament came to our rescue. With the boat swinging in the straps inches above the water, we learned how to repack and adjust a stuffing box.

After a short delay, John lowered us back into the water. We ran the engine a couple of hours to make sure there were no other problems.

By noon I shook John's hand, thanking him for all his help. He wished us good luck while untying our dock lines and we motored away. It was a mile to the mouth of the Chagrin River and into the waters of Lake Erie. Our maiden voyage would be a fifteen-mile trip west to Gordon Park.

We pre-paid a hundred-fifty dollar summer docking fee, getting a good spot on the left side of pier-one. Gordon Park shared a large yacht basin with, the Intercity Yacht Club and the Cleveland Municipal Boat Launching Ramps. The harbor entrance is well protected from the weather by two old lake freighters that were sunk and backfilled years ago.

We left the river and headed west parallel to the coast, staying about three-quarters of a mile offshore. With an unfavorable wind and choppy lake conditions, our speed of less than five knots was slower than expected.

I sat on the cabin roof with my feet on the forward deck. Kris stood at the controls, and Norm found a spot above him, sitting on the hard top.

We celebrated this first voyage with a six pack and a fat joint. As the mouth of the river disappeared into the shoreline behind us, we raised our beers, clinked the necks together and toasted the old carpenter. His dream made this day possible.

Clear skies, warm sunshine and the wind in my face, felt great. On my left, the beautiful rugged coastline of the eastern suburbs, to the right, the expanse of the lake. Our leisurely pace gave us the opportunity to enjoy the scenery, a chance to smell the roses. Beachfront property, wooded hills, and cliffs, blended in with the eroded backyards of upscale homes. There was a seemingly endless repeating pattern along the coast.

Off our starboard bow, a large beautiful ketch-rigged sailboat approach, all of fifty feet long with two masts and billowing sails. It was impressive. Pushed fast by the wind, it evoked a perspective of life I had never seen. A group of people at the stern waved as we passed. I returned the gesture.

Transitory vessels always acknowledge each other. It signified a kinship of which we were now included. The past four months I'd eagerly anticipated this day. It had finally arrived, and the world felt perfect.

That feeling quickly vaporized as the engine went silent. I ran to the rear hatch, Kris lifted it and I went in. It didn't take long to see that the fuel pump's glass inspection bowl was full of a brown substance instead of clear gasoline. Loose rust from our fifty-gallon fuel tank had worked its way into the filter, stopping its flow.

I shut the fuel valve and loosened the wing-nut to remove the glass filter. Using my index finger, I scooped the thick slurry out of the bowl. The task was complicated by our pitching and rolling hull. Without forward movement, the boat was at the mercy of the wind and waves.

The smell of gasoline and the constant jarring and rocking of the boat contributed to my queasiness. I had to prevail over the unpleasant feeling and finish the repair; stopping now would make things worse. Hell, it got worse by the second!

Repair finally finished, I crawled from the engine compartment and laid my head on the gunwale. Kris restarted the engine and we were underway again. Waves of nausea finally got the best of me as I heaved everything I had in my stomach. The steadiness of our forward motion and the breeze in my face hastened my recovery.

While disabled, the boat had been pushed by wind and waves and we were now farther from our destination. Our fuel problem returned a few hours later as the filter bowl clogged again. This time, Norm went into the engine compartment to clear the fuel obstruction. I talked him through the repair from up top in the fresh air. Rough seas caused Norm to drop the glass filter bowl and its gasket, which rolled under the engine to a difficult-to-retrieve location. The second repair took much longer. Seasickness finally overtook Norm, so I finished the job.

Headwinds and breakdowns were a pain-in-the-ass. Thankfully, after two or three more filter cleanings, the fuel tank ran out of loose rust. This issue behind us, we continued westward.

By dusk, another concern surfaced: our navigation lights were not yet working and we had no idea how much fuel remained of our original twenty gallons.

At last, in the distance, Norm spotted the red lights atop the four smokestacks of the Cleveland Electric Illuminating Company's coal burning plant at 55th Street. Our destination was 72nd Street, so Kris steered closer to shore where he spotted the Gordon Park entrance. The projected three hour trip took most of the day, but aside from the seasickness, it had been the most satisfying nine hours that I could recall. If we wanted to get places quickly, we'd have bought the speedboat.

CHAPTER 3: GORDON PARK

Motoring slowly into Gordon Park for the first time turned out to be one of those memorable moments that can best be described as described as bazaar.

We could see our new dock on the near side of the first pier. It lay ahead at the ten-o'clock position no more than two-hundred feet away. Two men stepped from a cabin cruiser on the far side of the pier acknowledging our arrival. They were told to expect us hours earlier. They waved; we responded.

A noticeable headwind greeted us as we slowly moved forward. The task at hand appeared simple, our new berth was actually close enough to hit with a rock. No one could have suspected such a simple task would take over half an hour completely entertaining for our inebriated observers.

Since I hadn't yet installed the linkage connecting the directional selector lever at the helm to the gearbox, we pre-planned a workaround. Norm stood on the bow handling dock lines. Kris, at the controls, would callout directional changes to me as I sat below, beside the gearbox with a flashlight in my mouth and two pipe wrenches. I made gear changes as directed.

Kris started yelling "Forward, neutral, forward, neutral, reverse, neutral, forward."

I tried my best to keep up with his callouts. Keep in mind, up to this point, our total experience operating a large boat consisted of the previous nine hours. Most of that time we traveled in a straight line and, of course, we had not yet experienced any of the *Day Tripper's* distinct handling traits. We didn't expect the headwind either; it complicated things.

I worked the pipe wrenches back and forth selecting directions. Above my head, steering cables moved frantically as Kris spun the wheel trying to stay in control. To my left, the engine raced and slowed as Kris struggled with the situation. He soon realized that the boat had almost no steering when going slow, so goosing the throttle was necessary to get directional water flowing past the rudder.

While all this was going on, Norm yelled steering suggestions to Kris, who in turn shouted directional changes to me. Our antics left no doubt of our nautical inability. To our audience, we must have looked like *The Three Stooges*.

Kris had never experienced the strong effect of crosswinds against our huge broadsided hull. We went this way, then that way, then this way, we zigzagged and circled, going everywhere but our intended path. The men on the pier howled with laughter. How silly we must have looked.

Finally, close enough for Norm and Kris to throw lines, the men pulled us the final ten feet to the pier.

Kris shut down everything as I emerged from the engine compartment covered with sweat. What a day this had been! Challenging but fun.

We thanked the men for their help and introduced ourselves. One of them, Hank, our new dockmate, greeted us by sucking back a swig from a silver hip flask. Then he passed it to Kris saying, "That was some entrance, Boss. Welcome to Gordon Park."

I was next and took a gulp, *HolyShit! What the hell did I just drink!* Norm was smart and passed on the swig after seeing my reaction.

Hank smiled and said, "It's Mescal, kinda like Tequila."

I'd never heard of Mescal before that, but killing that flask with Hank and his friend Warren, turned out to be a great way to begin a friendship.

Hank, a black man in his sixties, resembled a tall version of Sammy Davis Junior. He wore a white captain's cap and a blue blazer with a gold nautical crest on the breast pocket. Topsider boat shoes and white Bermuda shorts finished the ensemble. He looked every bit the part of a Captain. Hank proudly showed us his boat, a twenty-eight-foot *Lyman* cabin cruiser named the *Hanky Panky*. Like Hank, it was older but well maintained.

Over the next week we realized that a lot of beach-clad young women always hung-out around the *Hanky Panky*, Hank liked to have a good time and it showed.

He told us that although he was married, he played around a little. Owning a boat provided the perfect venue. He told us that after thirty-five years of marriage, he had an unspoken agreement with his wife; she accepted his *hussies* as long as they didn't interfere with their life at home or her family's occasional boat outing.

As I got to know Hank's wife, "*Mama*", I came to realize that their unspoken agreement was so unspoken, that Hank hadn't mentioned it to her. *Couldn't she see what he named the boat?*

Many nights, loud music and revelry aboard the *Hanky Panky* filled the air. It wasn't unusual to hear an occasional splash as a partygoer misjudged their footing and ended up in the water. Lots of drinking, lots of fun! The spillover from Hank's parties, at times, made their way across the eight-foot wide pier to the *Day Tripper*. Thus began a most-excellent, memorable summer.

* * *

Gordon Park Marina and Bait Shop were owned by a married couple named Junior and Della. They regularly worked hundred-hour weeks. Both tireless and smart, Junior and Della knew how to make a profit. Junior, short and stocky, had curly blond hair and crazy looking thick bushy eyebrows. Della, taller, bossy, and rotund, looked to be the real brains of the operation. I'd estimate their age to be the mid-thirties. We always got along well with both of them.

The Bait Shop occupied a 1000 square-foot red brick building. In the front, it shared a large city-owned parking lot with the municipal boat launching facility. The Bait Shop did a brisk business. It didn't hurt that its location was right next to the boat ramps, fishermen, and The Cleveland Shoreway, the freeway connecting the city to it's east and west suburbs.

On Junior's roof, a distinctive eight-foot-tall sign read: LIVE BAIT. If you drove by on the freeway, you saw that sign.

Gordon Park was a the seasonal home of forty watercraft, including Junior's sixteen aluminum rental fishing-boats and an assortment of private boats. Two commercial drift-fishing boats also called the marina home; the *Betty J* and the *Larson*. The largest pleasure craft was our thirty-five foot *Day Tripper*.

Junior, a true entrepreneur, knew how to make a good living through hard work. In addition to the marina, boat rentals, and Bait Shop, he owned a wholesale worm business. The worm farm, located in an attached twelve-by-fifteen-foot room behind the bait shop, housed and bred two types of worms. They were kept in large dirt-filled open-boxes that fit into frames reminiscent of big dresser drawers. Bright lights illuminated the room twenty-four-hours-a-day keeping the worms contained in their enclosures.

Junior had a guy who showed up every evening and packaged the worms into cardboard ice cream cup type cartons. Every morning, at dawn, live-bait dealers lined up to get a fresh supply of pre-packaged red worms and nightcrawlers for their customers.

In another endeavor, Junior ran daily advertisements in the classified section of the local papers. He offered to buy gold jewelry for cash, at around thirty-nine dollars an ounce.

He not only sold bait and tackle to the fishermen in the morning, but he had a fish scaling service when they returned with their catch. Scaling and cleaning, without a doubt, the worst part of fishing, made this a popular service. On a good day, a fisherman could easily catch ten to thirty perch, an abundant and delicious fish.

Junior's scaling machine did the job in five seconds for nine cents. Fish were fed tail-first into a slot in the top of the refrigerator-sized device, they emerged seconds later scales removed, from a chute at the bottom. One of Junior's helpers would then gut them for an additional five cents.

* * *

In the evening Gordon Park became a different place. The sounds, smells, and bustle of fishermen, pleasure boaters, and the launching ramps subsided.

Nighttime brought quiet and calm to the marina. Clanging halyards and the sound of gulls always relaxed me. A good time to read a book.

For me, the night was also a good time to cruise the waterfront. The bright lights of Cleveland's downtown office buildings contrast the dark sky over the lake. From Gordon Park to downtown, all but a half mile of the trip was within the calm waters inside the city's municipal breakwall. The breakwall, half a mile offshore, ran parallel to the coast protecting the waterfront from the lake when the weather gets nasty.

A gap in the breakwall downtown, at the Cuyahoga River allows navigable access to pleasure boats, freighters, tankers, and ore-boats. South of downtown, the river passes steel mills, refineries, and manufacturers, all awaiting the conveyance of materials.

* * *

The workday ended around nine for Junior and Della. They cleaned the property each night before locking the ten-foot chain-link security fence on their way out. A few boat owners, including us, had keys to the gate.

We slept aboard the *Day Tripper* most nights. I enjoyed staying overnight on the boat, the motion of the marina waters and the peaceful sounds put me right to sleep. At dawn, I'd awaken to the sounds of sea birds. No alarm clock necessary.

Kris and I worked for my father at his printed sportswear business downtown. It was only a ten-minute drive from the marina and we usually rode together to save parking costs. Norm also had a short drive to work at his family's transmission rebuilding service.

Some Saturday nights, Hank put together a poker game aboard his boat. The ten-dollar buy-in kept the game friendly and Hank's lively group of friends kept it entertaining, lots of drinks, joints, and laughs—good times.

Every now and then, Hank showed up with restaurant-sized carton of frozen ribs. His neighbor, a wholesale food delivery driver, would trade Hank ribs for an afternoon fishing trip. Hank liked to fish, so it was a win/win situation for all involved. If it wasn't for those occasional fishing trips, the *Hanky Panky* hardly ever left its slip.

One Saturday night, we threw a party at the marina. Hank supplied the main course and we provided a big *Weber* grill and plenty of charcoal. Back then a gallon of sauce, twenty-pounds of charcoal, and two gallons of potato salad sold for less than ten dollars at *Giant Tiger*. With our friends, Hank's friends and the marina people, we had a full-blown party going by the time Junior locked the gate.

It wasn't unusual for skyrockets, loud music, even a few celebratory gunshots, to entertain us long into the night. Loud noises were never a problem; the nearest homes were on the other side of the freeway past a hundred yards of thick woods. The *Day Tripper* and the *Hanky Panky* brought a new dynamic to Gordon Park, and everyone seemed to like it.

Marina-life suited me well. Although still technically living at my parents home, I was on my own for the first time and spending most nights at the marina. Each day I'd learn something new, meet new people, and did new things. We immersed ourselves into learning nautical rules, regulations, and protocol.

* * *

The *Day Tripper* had some distinct handling characteristics that we had yet to master. Our hull shape, big and broad, presented a lot of exposure to wind. At slower speeds, the boat's forward direction usually had to include compensation for the wind effect. That took a lot of practice, sometimes we'd spend all day taking turns docking and redocking.

The second issue that we had to deal with concerned backing. The boat pulled heavily to the right while going in reverse, regardless of the rudder position. Fortunately, the *Day Tripper* burned only a gallon of fuel an hour and gas was cheap; forty-cents a gallon. We spend many hours learning our boat's behaviors.

* * *

An hour's boat ride west of Gordon Park was one of our favorite, and most-visited, waterfront hangouts, *Captain Frank's Snack Bar*, located on the East 9th Street Pier, in downtown Cleveland. It was a popular place for boaters, motorists, and walk-up customers.

Their snack bar was located behind *Captain Frank's Lobster House*, a long established fine dining seafood institution. The snack bar offered casual drive-in style fast-food, and it was a busy place on warm summer evenings. A continuous band of round, yellow, bug-lights surrounded the parking lot and boat docks. After dark, the lights provided a carnival ambiance to the pier. With a high-end restaurant in the front and a snack bar in the back, the 9th Street Pier had something for every appetite.

In our first two months at the marina, we restored the *Day Tripper's* interior. New upholstery covered every soft surface and everything inside got a fresh coat of paint. Then came the big job - replacing the warped deck. None of us had any real experience with anything more complicated than building a doghouse. However, the job seemed straightforward: take the measurements, cut the wood, screw it down, done.

Fortunately, before we screwed it up (and we certainly would have), help came our way in the form of another new marina friend.

Junior let us know that he rented a slip on Pier Three to a guy with a classic mahogany speedboat, and he was a day late arriving.

"I'll keep an eye out for him," I said.

That night after Junior left, a boat that looked like a mahogany and chrome sculpture motored smoothly into the marina basin. I yelled to get the skipper's attention and pointed showing him where to tie-up. I went over to Pier Three to welcome him and help him with the lines.

He introduced himself as Ivan; he was twice our age but right from the start we connected. Ivan owned an impressive boat, a classic, fully restored, vintage 1920's Chris Craft mahogany speedboat.

Today, a boat like Ivan's, could could sell in the high six figures.

CHAPTER 4: CEDAR POINT

The time had come to replace the warped and weathered deck. Ivan, experienced in marine carpentry, offered to help us with the project. He not only knew the methods and materials, but he also had all the tools necessary to form the marine plywood into the shape of a deck.

Ivan, a hands-on adviser, showed up at the break of day, ready to work. With his guidance and tools, along with additional labor provided by friends, Bob and Perry, we laid, sealed and painted the new deck in only two weeks. It took all of our spare time, but the look of the boat went from shabby to shapely and when it rained, the deck didn't leak into the cabin anymore.

With the new deck in place, the *Day Tripper* not only looked beautiful, but it was now comfortable and dry. Being a double-ender, our boat had a unique old-school style and attracted a lot of attention.

Up to this point, all our out-of-pocket costs were still relatively low by boating standards. We had spent a total so far of under fifteen hundred dollars, quite the bargain. That included the cost of the boat itself, docking, and repairs. The restoration consumed nearly all our spare time, but the results were worth it. Now we could reap the fruits of our labor.

Ivan, an interesting and fun guy, introduced us to many new things, one of which was scuba diving. One morning he arrived at the marina with his three sets of scuba gear, saying "C'mon guys, I'm going to teach you to dive. Everything you need to know, I'll tell you on the ride out."

Oh hell yeah, scuba diving! That's something I had always wanted to do. One of my favorite childhood TV shows had been *Sea Hunt*. Now, here I was ready to enter the underwater world of *Mike Nelson*. Ivan gave us the most basic instructions and a few safety tips. He went in the water first, I followed.

I found myself twenty feet below the surface of Lake Erie looking up at the *Day Tripper*, a sight still fixed in my memory. The bottom of its big hull floated directly above my head, backlit by the noonday sun.

This unique perspective, at first, gave me an uncomfortable feeling, but it quickly gave way to an enjoyable and amazing experience. A bunch of little fish stared directly into my mask, *did they see their reflections as another group of fish?* When I turned my head, they followed, when I shooed them off, they returned. Ivan pointed out a big carp hiding next to a large rock.

I became aware of a strange thumping sound that got increasingly louder. LUB dub, LUB, dub,– the growing reverberations sounded like a fast heartbeat. What is making that noise? I looked at Ivan and he pointed up. We surfaced, I remembered his warning; exhale and ascend slower than your bubbles. Up top, we saw it! A huge tugboat passed by fifty yards away.

* * *

I always got a kick out of Ivan's heavy accent and broken English, it was peppered with strange phrases, and indecipherable words, he was a hoot. Ivan had an interesting early life in Yugoslavia, where he was jailed twice by the Communist government for trying to leave the country.

His dog accompanied him on his first attempt. Ivan stole a rowboat and under cover of darkness, tried to cross a river. The escape ended badly when an approaching patrol boat caused the dog to bark.

With an uneasy laugh, Ivan described the spotlight shining on him while he held the dog in a headlock trying to hold its mouth shut. After his arrest, he spent a year locked in a prison work camp.

Upon being released, he tried to leave the country again, that time hiding inside a crate on a truck. The driver got scared and sold Ivan out. That second arrest earned him eighteen more months in confinement.

Still determined to leave, he finally succeeded the third time by walking out through the forest. His destination, eventually Cleveland, where he'd heard he had an uncle. For two years, Ivan worked aboard freighters, saw the world and saved his money.

Then he set out to try and find his relative. Aside from knowing his uncle's name, his only other clue: he was probably in Cleveland. Ivan came to town and found a large Yugoslavian community who were willing to help him. Through word of mouth and many door-to-door encounters, Ivan finally found his uncle. It was the first time they ever met and his uncle invited Ivan to come live with his family. Through study and hard work, Ivan became a mechanical engineer. He married, raised a family and fulfilled his American dream.

Years later, Ivan became the patriarch of an extended family that included his Puerto Rican wife, three kids, a mother-in-law, two sisters-in-law, and their kids, they all lived in his large, three-family home. Ivan's family lived on the second floor, his in-laws lived above and below him. Multi-family dwellings were common in Cleveland's neighborhoods. All had full basements and some, like Ivan's, had finished attic apartments.

With all the women and kids running around his house, Gordon Park was a respite for him. He went there almost as much as we did. Now and then his wife also needed a break from family and joined him at the marina. Whenever she visited, she brought a big thermos of coffee and delicious homemade snacks.

* * *

After months of work, the boat was ready for its inaugural shakedown cruise. Our destination would be Cedar Point, a large amusement park and marina complex sixty miles west, in Sandusky Bay. We'd go over the upcoming Fourth-of-July holiday.

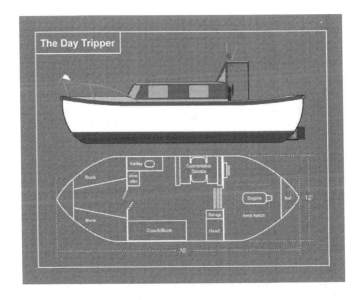

When I told my parents about our plan, my mother made me promise to wear a lifejacket and call her when we departed and when we arrived. She felt nervous about our lack of experience and our fifty dollar boat. I assured her I would not forget to call, and that I would always wear a life jacket. *Yeah, right!*

We left for Cedar Point after work on Tuesday the second of July. Bob and Perry joined us for this first trip. We looked forward to a few days of fun and sun. When we stopped at the Cleveland Yacht Club to fill our fuel tank, I spotted a pay phone and ran to call my mother. She reminded me again to call her the moment we got to Cedar Point.

I looked at my watch; it was close to nine and starting to get dark. The trip could take up to twelve hours. We'd navigate visually hugging the coastline while traveling westward. Since we did not yet have a compass, the coast, lit by the moon, guided us to Cedar Point.

Heading out the western cut (opening) of the breakwall, Norm noticed a dim light beam off to our right. It repeated a pattern of three short flashes, not quite an SOS, but worth a short detour to investigate. We found a small powerboat, near the big breakwall rocks, signaling us with a nearly dead flashlight. Aboard were three seasick, drunk people. Their engine had flooded, and the waves were about to push them into the jagged rocks of the breakwall. We had to act fast. Norm jumped onto their bow and secured a tow line, we pulled them to safety and towed the boat to the nearby Edgewater Yacht Club, a little out of our way, but we probably saved three lives. By the time they were situated, it was late, so we spent the night in an open slip and resumed our trip in the morning.

We cruised a little further offshore where the coast dipped southward for twenty miles. Still about three or four miles from land, we could easily see land. Everything went well until a shear pin on the prop shaft broke.

There is a coupling designed to break if the prop strikes a solid object, thus saving the prop by sacrificing the shear pin. I originally used a thick nail to join the coupling; it turned out to be a poor substitute for a real pin. The nail proved to be too soft of a metal and broke easily under full power. I replaced the sheared nail with another one, since it was all we had. By reducing our power setting for the duration of the trip, we'd put less strain on the nail.

During the time we focused on our mechanical problem, the sky became heavily overcast and an offshore breeze pushed us out of sight of land. Without visual references or a compass, we had no idea which direction to proceed.

Engulfed in a cloud bank, with low visibility, we quickly realized we were in trouble. Our line-of-sight navigation method had failed us. Without a view of the coast, the plan went to shit real fast. My immediate concern, if we drifted or motored in the wrong direction, we might head away from shore and into the shipping lanes to the north.

While we discussed our options, Bob snapped his fingers, saying something no one understood as he darted into the cabin and opened our tool/junk drawer, he dug through its familiar contents.

Bob had helped us with the deck the previous week and he'd been in that drawer many times, he seemed to know exactly what he was looking for. Bob found a magnet, a wine cork, and took a sewing needle from our First Aid kit. He magnetized the needle by stroking it across the magnet, then floating it on the piece of cork in a glass of water, the needle pointed north! We had a compass.

Bob remembered seeing the experiment on the old *Watch Mister Wizard* television series, and he put the trick to good use. I pointed the bow south-west towards shore, soon we came out of the fog.

With the coastline back in view, I turned west and was careful to stay in clear sight of land. By the time we passed the city of Lorain, the weather changed to sunny and clear.

Along the way, we found ourselves in the middle of a big sailboat race. They overtook us, so we held our course as they quietly passed at twice our speed. I found it exciting and beautiful seeing their big colorful spinnaker sails billowing in the breeze.

The trip to Cedar Point took longer than expected. We finally entered Sandusky Bay after dark on Wednesday, July third. It had been twenty-four hours since we left Gordon Park Marina.

I tied up at the fuel dock and headed for the office. Being a holiday weekend and our reservation twelve hours late, I hoped we'd still get a slip.

We were lucky and got the last available spot that could accommodate our length. The space, located at the far edge of the marina was not normally used, but it was available and we were happy to have it.

As it turned out, our slip was right next to the girls' dormitories. The amusement park hired college students and housed them in large dorm buildings. On subsequent visits, we always requested that slip at the back-edge of the marina.

At dawn, we were awakened by someone pounding hard on the hull and calling my name, "Leonard Berman, Leonard Berman!"

I opened the door, seeing two young Coast Guardsmen. One asked if I was Leonard Berman, his mood seemed unpleasant. Just then it hit me—shit, I forgot to call my mother!

Last night she called the Coast Guard and reported us twelve hours overdue. The Guardsman told me they spent the night trying to locate us on the lake. I thanked him, saying "I was sorry for their inconvenience, I'll go call her right now."

He said, "Hold on, I'm required to give you a safety inspection."

We had all the stuff: life jackets, flares, fire extinguishers and a clean flame suppressor, but the one thing we didn't have was a *suitable* bell. Our bicycle bell didn't suffice.

Before the Guardsman wrote us an equipment violation, I convinced him to let me go to the marina store and buy a bell, he agreed. Norm and I ran to the store and found the only bell available, it was an eight-inch, solid brass model that sold for sixty dollars. That was all our extra money.

Norm ran the new bell back to the boat to show the Guardsman, and I called my mother from a pay phone. I explained our delay and apologized for not calling her when we arrived. I was truly sorry that my mistake caused her and my dad so much unnecessary overnight grief.

* * *

We could no longer afford to go to the amusement park, but the trip, as a whole, ended up being lots of fun. We invited a group of girls from the dorms to go for a boat ride around Sandusky Bay. The girls hung around till noon and returned after work each night. One of them brought along her guitar, We had a great time and I discovered that I should never sing in public again.

We'd head back to Cleveland in a few days with our new brass bell that cost more than the boat.

***

On the trip home, beautiful weather and excellent lake conditions prevailed. By dawn we were already on our way, I hoped we'd make Cleveland before dark. Alone at the controls, there was a certain serenity in the stillness of the water disturbed only by our wake, as far as I could see, we were the only boat in sight.

I thought about that day six months ago, when I first climbed the rickety ladder from under the hull and stepped aboard the boat for the first time. I saw myself standing in this exact spot and imagined this scenario. Goosebumps rose on my forearms.

Four hours earlier, the party ended and the girls left. I fell asleep on the rear deck in a folding aluminum chaise lounge. Waking before first light, I looked into the open cabin door. The guys were crashed-out, two were in bunks, two on the floor and empty beer cans filled the spaces between them.

After running the bilge blower, I started the engine, untied the dock lines and lifted the bumpers. Easing open the throttle the boat began to move forward, and we were on our way home. The still morning air and calm water made it easy to handle the departure without any help. To the morning marina sounds, I slowly guided the *Day Tripper* out of Cedar Point. The sun, now barely above the horizon, felt good on my face.

Around ten, the cabin door opened and a disheveled and squinting Perry came out into the bright sunshine. Shielding his eyes, he asked, "Where are we?"

"Not quite to Lorain. You don't look too good."

"I feel like shit," Perry groaned as he headed to the stern to throw up. Then he went forward and sat on the bow.

A short time later, Bob came out and relieved himself off the stern, "Norm was in the head and I couldn't wait," he explained.

Kris half-crawled out of the cabin, got to his feet and asked "Why didn't you wake me? I'd have given you a hand with the boat."

"No need, I handled it, we've been underway for almost four hours."

Norm brought out five cups of instant coffee, a stale loaf of white bread, and half a jar of peanut butter, the last of our food supply.

Bob took the wheel, I went below to wash-up and change into swim trunks. Someone already neatened-up the cabin and opened the windows, probably Norm.

Those days, our best defense against sunburn was a good-old basic tan. The three of us were already tanned and used to the summer sun. But, Perry and Bob, who did some sunbathing yesterday, were a little on the pink side. On the trip home, they relied on sunburn cream to ease their pain.

By late afternoon we had already replaced the shear-pin/nail three times. Buying an actual shear-pin will be our first priority, a compass our second. Aside from the pin issues, the shakedown cruise proved the boat to be seaworthy and safe.

Back in local waters, Gordon Park was a welcome sight; three nights of partying with the dorm girls had worn us out. We were tired and hungry. After securing the boat we went our five separate ways. The only thing on my mind was a decent meal and a long hot shower.

CHAPTER 5: STASH

We bought our weed from a friend of Kris', a guy named "Stash". He'd delivered pot to the boat a few times and we always asked him to join us on one of our fishing trips. Stash had never fished before but said he like try it one day. I convinced him to join us the following Saturday morning.

His nickname Stash, fit him well. He had a big thick mustache that always reminded me of *Wyatt Earp* or *Super Mario*. I never knew Stash's real name, but in his profession, it was better that way.

Stash, always friendly and polite, referred to most people as "My friend," and added that phrase to his greetings, "Nice to see you, my friend," like that.

Stash always traveled with his big, well trained, German Shepherd guard-dog named Dutch. I swear that dog understood English as well as most people. I never saw Dutch exhibit any aggressive behavior to anyone, but I had no doubt he had the capacity if commanded. We were asked not to ever give treats or food scraps to Dutch. We didn't.

Stash had a big gray Chevy van which he drove back and forth to Florida every few months. He'd pick up fifty to a hundred pounds of weed, usually Colombian Gold, on each trip.

Stash never sold or used any other drugs but grass, which he said came from the Earth. Stash and his longtime girlfriend, Donna, were highly spiritual, holistic long haired hippy types. They spent a month each year, living in a commune near California's Big Sur. *"Giving back,"* is how Stash referred to it

The price of "weed," those days was a bargain at twenty dollars an ounce. Pot, back then, had seeds that had to be separated out and removed by hand. If a seed got into a joint it could explode like a kernel of popcorn, and that wasn't good. A couple of my t-shirts had little burn holes from seeds that were left in joints. Preparing the weed was a bit of a process, but it was well worth the time.

As Stash and his dog came aboard he told us he hadn't been on a boat since he came to America, as an eight-year-old. "I think you're going to have fun," I told him, "Perch are about the easiest fish to catch. If they're biting, we'll do well."

It couldn't have been a better afternoon. Everyone caught fish, we smoked Stash's personal weed and drank his red wine. Back at the marina after cleaning and filleting the fish, we had plenty to go around.

Ivan, his friend Mateo and Hank joined us for dinner. After a delicious meal at the picnic table, we moved the party over to the privacy of the *Hanky Panky*, where Stash said he had a special treat for us. It was a *Thai-Stick*. None of us ever had heard of a *Thai-Stick*.

Stash went to his van and returned holding a two-foot tall bamboo bong. From his pocket, he produced what looked like a thick, six-inch, light-green twig. Upon closer inspection, you could see the *Thai-Stick* was made from small clusters of marijuana buds tied tightly around a thin bamboo central twig. A fibrous plant thread held it all in place. The stick had a strong distinct sweet smell and a sticky crystalline surface. I'd estimate its width to be just under an inch. *So this was a Thai-Stick.*

Stash took off a small chunk, broke it up and loaded the bong bowl. He turned to us and said "This will fuck you up, my friend. Just take one deep hit."

Holding his lit Zippo over the bowl, he offered me the first toke. I inhaled and held it in as long as I could. Then, I coughed out a large white thick cloud of smoke. The rest of the group followed my lead. Even Mateo, who hadn't ever smoked pot, gave it a try.

Hank poured everyone a shot and we all drank-it-down. Soon the *Thai-Stick* kicked in. At first, I noticed my eyes tracked movement differently. Colors were more distinct and the fabric of my blue jeans looked to be moving around slightly. Sgt. Pepper's Lonely Hearts Club Band played on the radio, yet the music sounded unusual.

We all laughed and whooped it up for who knows how long, then we realized Mateo wasn't on the boat. Ivan went to look around and he called us out to the pier where Mateo's clothes were left in a trail going up the pier steps.

After a short search, we found him naked and kneeling behind the bait-shop. He was running water from a hose spigot over his head in a constant flow. He kept saying "I'm alright, I'm alright."

While we walked him back to the boat, he told us he may have inhaled too much smoke, we all laughed like it was the funniest joke we ever heard, including Mateo.

A while later with a huge case of the mass-munchies, we fired up the *Day Tripper* and all of us headed to *Captain Frank's*. The boat ride to the snack bar was highlighted by the twinkling lights of the city and loud rock and roll blasting on our radio.

On the more subdued return trip, everyone but Stash and I had already crashed-out. I let him steer the boat all the way back to the marina, then he helped me with the dock lines. As he left the boat, he put his hand on my shoulder and said, "I've had a great time, my friend.

CHAPTER 6:
55TH STREET MARINA

Junior said there was a military surplus store on the west side of town where he recently saw a compass for sale. "They got a lot of good stuff," he said.

He was right; they had everything from bombsights to gas masks including five or six compasses. Most of them were too large, but they did have one three inch marine compass for twelve dollars, I bought it for ten. A little paint and it was good as new.

To resolve our shear pin issue, Norm and I removed the coupling from the drive shaft and took it to a machine shop. They took some measurements and sold us a simple device called a roll-pin. I think it cost a buck. Problem solved.

After work on Friday, we met at the boat as usual. With the weekend ahead and a rainy few days behind us, the forecast called for sunny skies. Bob, his girlfriend, Mary, and three of her girlfriends all planned to join us at noon tomorrow. We'd fish, sunbathe, and barbeque.

* * *

Next to us on the *Hanky Panky*, Hank leaped from his chair, pumping his fist in the air and yelling "Yesssssss! Yes! Yessss!"

He had been listening to the ball game, with a couple friends. The Indians had won in extra innings. He was an avid baseball fan.

Heading to *Captain Frank's* for dinner, we looked forward to the crowds and post-game celebrations.

Captain Frank's, a quarter mile east of Cleveland's baseball Stadium, could expect lots of happy fans in their lounge, restaurant, and snack bar. There'd be fun times downtown tonight and we were on our way.

Upon arrival, we circled the pier looking for a place to dock; there was none. After a short wait, a couple smaller boats docked together left and we claimed the spot. It looked like it would be a tight fit. Kris nosed up to the pier and I jumped off holding the bow line which I secured to a bollard, ready to slacken and tighten as needed. Since the *Day Tripper* backed only towards the right, we used that characteristic to our advantage whenever we could. This was one of those times. I was able to form a pivot point using a spring line technique and we maneuvered the boat into a spot barely longer than our hull. Essentially we parallel parked a thirty-five-foot boat.

"Let me give you a hand," said someone on the boat ahead, as he jumped onto the pier and ran over to help.

He tied the aft line as I adjusted our dock bumpers, "Thanks." I said.

The guy looked to be in his late thirties, wearing worn blue jeans and an old Cleveland Indians sweatshirt. He introduced himself as Ralph, and guessed that our boat was originally a lifeboat, he recognized it from his Navy days.

We talked for a few minutes and he asked if he could come aboard and have a look around.

"Hell yeah," I said, always happy to show off the *Day Tripper*.

Ralph, a boating enthusiast, seemed to like what he saw. He invited us to join him aboard his boat. It was a sixty-foot custom-built *Chris Craft*

Constellation. One beautiful yacht.

Everything about it exudes luxury: polished mahogany, brass, marble, teak and white leather abound. I had no idea that boats as nice as this even existed. The words holy shit, came to mind when I stepped into the massive main salon.

He introduced us to his group, his girlfriend, and two other guys then pointed us to the bar.

"Help yourselves, boys."

Ralph gave us the grand-tour. The main cabin was enormous and furnished in classic formal style. Forward of the salon, we stepped down to a galley, two private cabins, two bathrooms and six bunks. The main stateroom, under the rear deck, looked like a luxury hotel suite and was almost as big.

His vessel had been designed by a marine architect, and built by *Chris Craft*; only two of this same design were made.

Ralph, an ex-Clevelander, and a big Indians fan cruised down from Detroit with his group to watch the ball game. He also planned to visit his parents while in town.

We sat around shooting the shit for a while, then Kris went to the snack bar for a pack of cigarettes. He returned with three good-looking girls. They were new to Cleveland and lived at the Job Corps dorms.

The girls were downtown to watch their first Major League baseball game. All three were from Kentucky. Kris met them at the snack bar and invited them to join us aboard the yacht. *Just when I thought the night couldn't get any better, it got better.*

Around midnight, we invited the girls to go for a boat ride on our boat. We said our goodbyes to Ralph and friends, thanked them for a fun evening, and headed over to the *Day Tripper*.

It was calm inside the breakwall on that warm summer night. Kris was at the wheel, his new friend by his side, the other girls paired-up with me and Norm, and we all sat on the cabin top. We were just getting cozy when a loud blast from our new air horns startled the hell out of us.

I turned quickly to see a topless girl steering the boat, *nothing wrong with that.* Behind her, Kris stood with a big smile and a joint dangling from the corner of his mouth.

We headed to the new, almost finished, 55th Street Marina. It was dark and secluded, the perfect place to continue our party. We tied up at one of the new floating docks, we were the only vessel in the 360-boat facility.

It didn't take long before the night watchman appeared on the dock beside us. "We won't be open until the end of the month," said the watchman. "You'll have to leave."

Kris stepped onto the dock and talked to him for a minute, then went into the cabin and came out with a paper bag holding three beers. As quietly as he appeared, the watchman vanished.

For the rest of the night, we swam, drank, danced and partied. As the rising sun lit the eastern sky, I started the engine, released the dock lines, and we headed back to Gordon Park.

Once at the dock, I drove the girls to the Job Corps dorms where they expected curfew violations.While driving back to the boat, I remembered Bob and four girls would be there at noon. I hoped for a couple of hours' sleep before they arrived. If things worked out right, it could be another long night. *What the hell, I can always sleep on Sunday.*

CHAPTER 7:
THE GLENVILLE RIOTS

While Detroit, Washington D.C., New York, Baltimore, and Chicago erupted in riots, Cleveland remained relatively calm. It was due in part to the leadership of Mayor Carl B. Stokes. He recently become the first black mayor of a major American city.

It all started on a hot evening in late July, shots were fired on a narrow street in the Glenville neighborhood of Cleveland's racially charged East Side. It turned into a full-scale gun battle between police and snipers. An hour and a half later, seven people were dead including three policemen. Fifteen others were wounded in the confrontation.

Violence, rioting, and aggression against police and fire department responders ensued. For their safety, Mayor Stokes pulled them off the streets in the stricken neighborhoods. Ohio Governor, Jim Rhodes, ordered the National Guard to restore order to the streets.

The Guard patrolled Glenville and adjacent neighborhoods in Jeeps, most with mounted machine guns and three-man crews. The Glenville neighborhood, less than a mile from Gordon Park, was too close for comfort. With all the reports of looting and vandalism, Junior boarded up the bait shop sales counter that faced the large city parking lot. Then he locked the big chain-link fence surrounding the marina.

Junior and Della decided to stay on the property and protect their business from looters. They were well prepared; Junior had an M1 Garand army rifle and Della wore a .45 automatic on her hip, keeping her 12-gauge pump shotgun nearby.

The three of us decided to stay on the boat. We'd worked so hard to get to this point, we weren't about to turn and run. Stocking up on supplies and food, we were ready for anything. I bought my .38 snub-nose from home. Kris and Norm brought their guns and we were ready to stand with Junior and Della.

Hank, who lived in Glenville, sent his family to the safety of the suburbs before coming to the marina. "Nobody going to fuck with the *Hanky Panky*," said Hank, arriving with an M1 Carbine, a metal ammo box, and his armed friend, Warren.

Ivan came prepared with two high-powered hunting rifles and a 9-millimeter pistol. His family had been temporarily sent to stay with relatives on the west side.

About ten of us remained in the marina, plus Junior and Della. Della told everyone that they appreciate their help and support in the face of adversity.

The tall fence around the property had been locked and chained shut. To provide a more secure position, Ivan instructed us to form a barrier line inside the fence using our cars. They could shield us in case anyone tried to shoot towards the marina, or ram the gate.

After dark, gunshots in the distance were frequent and unnerving. The air smelled of smoke and fire, and when the wind shifted, it stung our eyes. To the south, the night sky flickered with light from neighborhood fires.

After midnight, Ivan rallied us all together when he saw a truck pull up and stop about twenty-five yards outside the fence. Six to eight men got out and stood together talking while pointing toward the marina. Through his binoculars, Ivan saw at least two of the men had guns, and others carried crow-bars or pipes.

We guessed they intended to loot the boats but may have had second thoughts after seeing that we were prepared. Ivan told us if they advance, he'd take the first shot and shoot out their windshield. We should hold our fire and give them a chance to retreat.

"If they keep coming do what you can to stop them," said Ivan.

I had Ivan's 300 *Weatherby* Magnum rifle at the ready. We stayed silent and watched them; they kept talking. Three minutes, ten minutes, who knows? Time dragged, what were they going to do?

Then, Della, by my side, chambered a round into her .45 and pumped a shell into her shotgun. Those two unmistakable metallic sounds did not go unnoticed by the truck-group. They jumped over each other getting into the truck-bed as it sped away with its lights off. We rotated sentry duty the next two evenings. Fortunately, there were no other incidents at the marina.

CHAPTER 8: RAT FISHING

By August, Cleveland calmed down and things returned to normal. We began to notice that more rats than usual were hanging around Junior's growing pile of fish scales. Because of complaints Junior agreed to remove it as soon as he had a chance. Meanwhile, we decided to take the matter into our own hands. We'd use our BB guns to help control the rodent population.

The pile, next to the scaling machine, was about fifty feet from the end of our pier, a good shooting distance for BB guns. Rats, it turned out, were not that easy to hit at night.

We even tried rat-fishing. We'd bait a tiny treble hook with salami and cast it over near the pile. When a rat took the bait we'd set the hook and reel him in; a BB would finish him off. Hank and his friends saw what we were doing and joined in. That first night we killed over a dozen rats. The following night we killed only half that number, and soon no rat would bite a baited hook.

I'm convinced the rats somehow communicated, warning each other about the fish hooks. We went back to BB guns but added a spotlight beam from Hank's boat. It didn't take long to gain control of the rat population.

Around that same time, I ran into an old high school buddy at a house party. He gave me two skyrockets left over from the fourth of July. They weren't the type that made the big colorful aerial displays, they were the ones that exploded with a humongous boom and a huge white flash. Its blast was so large and loud, that you felt the shockwave of pressure slam against your body.

The skyrockets were big. A red foot-long cylinder had an attached three-foot launching stick. A label around the center identified it as Super-Thunder One Thousand. The first rocket launched perfectly and produced a huge explosion about three hundred feet above our heads.

The second rocket had a broken stick, so I made a hasty repair with masking tape, set the rocket in the launch tube, lit the fuse, and jumped back.

When the rocket launched, my tape repair failed. With only half a tail stick for stabilization, the skyrocket did a couple of speedy loops above our heads. Then it turned towards the ground and with a large "whump," disappeared deep into the center of Junior's five-foot-tall pile of fish-scales!

Everyone ran for cover. I jumped behind a car just as the explosion went off. Louder than anything I had ever heard, my ears went temporarily deaf. I stood up with my ears ringing, then realized glittery fish scales were floating down around me. It looked like the inside of a shaken snow-globe. *Oh shit! This is going to make a big damn mess.*

Junior arrived at daybreak and saw the aftermath of the fish scale explosion, he had questions. Someone pointed him to the *Day Tripper*.

Not yet six o'clock in the morning, Junior slapped the side of our hull a couple of times to wake us. As I expected, he wasn't happy. You know the saying "It looked like a bomb went off." Well, in the daylight, you could actually see the radial blast pattern of scales and it looked exactly like a bomb went off.

We spent the rest of the day cleaning the scales from all of Junior's rental boats along with the bait shop roof, yard, and a few other vessels.

Della laughed and said, "In the words of Ghoulardi, from now on, *cool it with the boom-booms.*"

CHAPTER 9: OUR NEW BOW RAIL

On a beautiful summer night while on a date with Linda from the Job Corp, we sat and talked at our picnic table near the pier. I had taken her to see the movie *Rosemary's Baby*, then we went to the marina for a couple beers. The night went well, so I said in my most convincing manner "Instead of going home, you should stay on the boat. I'll take you to the dorm before dawn."

Negotiations going well, I'd almost persuaded her to stay, when a bright flash over the lake lit the sky. An undulating amber light now glowed on the horizon. We jumped atop the picnic table for a better view, just as a thunderous "booooom" echoed past the coastline and rumbled through the city.

Hank, alerted by the sound, came out of his cabin wearing a bathrobe, behind him a female companion took a look around and went back inside. Hank sat in his captain's chair and turned on the marine radio.

A few minutes later, he shouted "A large cruiser exploded and it's still burning. People are assisting, and the Coast Guard's on the way."

He quickly returned to his cabin.

From our vantage point on the table, we could see the flashing red light of the Coast Guard cutter as it closed the wide gap to the burning boat. People in the marina were up-and-about, trying to find out what happened. With all the excitement, the mood had passed with my date and I took Linda to her dorm. I admit it, I was disappointed, but I hoped to see her again.

Early the next morning, I heard a commotion and stepped out to investigate. I saw the remains of the previous evening's excitement, a large burned out steel hull was towed into the marina. Yesterday it was a beautiful boat, now it's reduced to a charred mess. Little remained above the gunwale, but it did have a nice bow rail. I watched for a while as a small tugboat maneuvered the hull into one of Junior's empty slips.

The tugboat skipper and a couple of guys were talking to Junior. A few minutes later they shook hands and left, leaving the charred hull behind.

I walked to the bait shop and spoke to Junior, "What's up with the burned boat? It's an eyesore."

"They can leave that thing in my marina as long as they want," said Junior. "They're paying $50 a day for the slip. I don't care if it sits there the rest of the summer."

We paid $150 for the whole season, so he was doing well on that slip. Junior walked away laughing to himself. He was rubbing his thumb against his fingers, in the give-me-money gesture, saying "*Recompense me, recompense me. That was the happiest I'd ever seen Junior.*"

Channel Eight TV News reported that twelve people survived, but one man was missing. A company party held aboard the rented forty-eight-foot yacht ended with the explosion and fire.

The newscast showed a video of the burned boat in Gordon Park and, there in the background, the *Day Tripper* made its TV début.

Junior later told us the insurance inspector determined that a build-up of gasoline fumes in the bilge probably caused the explosion. The bilge-blower switch was in the off position and the ignition switch was on.

Boats with gasoline engines must always purge their bilge prior to starting. It looked to the inspector, that this step had been missed.

A couple weeks later, Junior told us a scrap metal company would be coming for the hull. Junior's cash-cow would be leaving. He'd made almost a thousand dollars in dock fees, so he was happy. In fact, he was in such a good mood he offered Kris and me, free popsicles, a rare gesture and genuinely appreciated on that hot afternoon.

But before the burned hull was gone, we noticed, the boat, had a nice-looking, undamaged, albeit soot-covered, stainless steel bow rail. It looked like it would fit nicely on the front of the *Day Tripper*. So, late that night we removed the rail and hid it in the water beneath our boat. In the unlikely event that somebody inquired about the rail, it just might mysteriously show up.

CHAPTER 10: NAVIGATING

Now that we had a compass and local navigation charts, we were anxious to use them. Deciding on another trip to Cedar Point was a no-brainer, we loved the place. Kris couldn't make the trip, but Bob's younger brother, Danny, came along.

Leaving Gordon Park at twilight on a moonless night, Norm would be first at the wheel. Danny sat on the cabin roof providing an extra set of eyes to scan ahead on this dark night.

Instead of following the coastline, we headed northwest for a exactly two hours, at six-knots that should put us around fourteen- miles out. Then we'd turn to a direct heading to Sandusky Bay. We'd shave two hours off our trip, but more importantly, we did some real navigation. I looked forward to being out of sight of land for nearly the whole trip. If all went as expected, our new compass and chart would get us there. I'd estimate the compensation for wind.

I went below for a two-hour snooze before relieving Norm. I fell asleep easily in the forward cabin. The sounds of the bow plowing through the water, combined with the constant drone of the engine, put me right out.

Next thing I knew, Danny tugged at my shoe saying, "It's time to switch with Norm. You said to wake you in two hours."

In the dark cabin, I splashed some water on my face before opening the door and stepping out into what I can only describe as the most spectacular view I had ever seen.

Devoid of light pollution, the sky was a continuous blanket of stars. I stood there motionless as I took it all in. Directly above, the cloud-like arms of the Milky Way, the *Great Rift*, reached across the sky. It looked clear and distinct. *Where has this view been all my life? I've looked at the night sky a million times before and never saw anything like this.*

Given this new perspective, and a moment to ponder, I realized how minuscule we actually were in this universe. Every star I could see was millions of times larger than Earth, so many stars, so many. I looked at Norm and he said: "Blows your mind, doesn't it."

I relieved him at the wheel and we turned to 255°. With the dark, flat lake ahead and the entire universe above, we pressed on through the night at a constant six-knots. If everything went as I planned, Sandusky Bay would be fifty miles dead ahead. Aside from a single sighting of a lake freighter, far to the north, Norm, Danny, and I were about as alone as three people could be.

The next morning, as the glow of the rising sun climbed in the sky behind us, I spotted two faint lights on the dark forward horizon. Grabbing my binoculars and checking the chart, the two lights were unmistakable. Marblehead to the north, and the Sandusky Harbor light, directly off our bow! I identified the Marblehead light by its green flash every six seconds.

We'd done it. Danny pulled out a joint as thick as a finger from his shirt pocket. *How the hell do you roll them that big? I wondered,* as I drew-in deep and long.

* * *

That first night at the marina, Danny stayed behind with a girl he'd met. Norm and I headed to the amusement park. First, we rode the roller coasters and go-karts; later ending up on the midway. Shooting galleries, darts, skeeball and sideshows entertained us until closing.

Walking back to the marina through a thick fog, the *Day Tripper* came into view. I could make out Danny sitting on the cabin roof. He held a beer in one hand, and… what the hell? His other hand was wrapped up like a huge Q-tip. Danny's explanation: he'd picked up a dud firecracker and blew into the end.

Aside from a couple of sore fingers, no serious injury had occurred—his huge wrapped hand, the result of an over-zealous good Samaritan who came to his aid with way too much gauze.

The next morning brought a steady drizzle and grey skies. The air in the cabin felt hot and heavy and I'd only been awake an hour. I drank the last can of warm pop on the boat then walked to the store to pick up some groceries. The drizzle turned out to be a refreshing change from the hot, torpid air in the cabin. *The next thing this boat needs is a damn fan.*

I picked-up peanut butter, bread, a case of soda, and a couple bags of chips. We were good for another day or two. The rain ceased, but humidity lingered. We fanned ourselves with magazines trying to keep cool, that worked for a little while. Finally, late in the afternoon, a breeze brought relief from the muggy air.

That evening, the fellow in the sailboat docked ahead of us, asked if we wanted to join him, his wife, and their guests, to play some penny-a-point rummy. Norm and I accepted. His two guests were visiting from Buenos Aires; they spoke only Spanish. In spite of that barrier, we had a fun interesting little party. Five-Hundred-Rummy transcends all languages.

Before leaving their boat, I listened to the latest marine weather forecast. A storm front headed this way would be here in approximately 24 hours. Norm and I agreed, unless a small-craft advisory was posted, we'd head home at sunrise.

In the morning, a light rain fell as we passed the Sandusky Harbor Lighthouse. Now, out of the calmer bay and with two hours travel behind us, the lake ahead began to churn with choppy whitecaps. As we put on our life jackets, Danny mumbled a prayer and crossed himself. That was the first religious thing I'd ever seen him do, and I'd known him since he was four.

The boat had been in foul weather before but always close to home. This time fifty miles of rough water lay ahead. Should we turn back? This would be the time to do it. I pondered the choice, but my confidence in the boat prevailed and we pressed ahead

.

The rainfall increased as the morning progressed, and choppy whitecaps turned into two-foot swells. The deck pitched and rolled as I moved with it, rocking at my hips to counter the motion. Norm and I had our sea-legs, but Danny, not used to being on a boat, didn't do well. At some point, Norm braced him at the rail to keep him from being pitched overboard while he retched, again and again.

The storm appeared on the eastern horizon, more than twelve hours before its predicted arrival. Through my binoculars, I saw flashes inside the storm clouds. "Lightning. Oh shit," I said, as a shiver rose up my spine.

Horror stories of lightning striking boats were legendary, but were they credible? I didn't know, nor did I want to find out. Any way you look at it, a boat is not the best place to be in an electrical storm.

I changed our course and headed for the closest port, Lorain Harbor, fifteen miles to the southeast. Under better conditions, it would be a two-hour trip. We'd find sanctuary in the Black River where taller structures would protect us from the storm.

I opened the throttle that last inch to muster every bit of power that our engine could provide. We were heading to port as fast as we could go. With me at the controls, Norm at my side, and Danny lying spread-eagled on the rear deck, I hoped like hell we'd beat the storm to Lorain.

No one spoke that last couple of hours. I think we all knew, the outcome was out of our hands. Steering now towards the Lorain Lighthouse beacon, I could see the storm to the east, closing fast. I swallowed hard, cleared my throat, and re-cinched the straps on my life-jacket.

A mile short of the harbor entrance the storm hit us hard and I lost sight of the Lighthouse. High winds and heavy rain slowed our progress. The squall obscured my vision as I struggled to stay on course. The wind and waves pushed us westward. To maintain control, I pointed the bow east, directly into the blinding storm. There was no way to tell if we were making forward progress, or not. Sheets of rain blew into my face, I couldn't see shit. Then, like the guiding light that it is, the Lorain Lighthouse beacon revealed itself again through the storm.

The bad news—we were too far west. We had to be east of the lighthouse to enter the harbor. A long angular city breakwall connected the lighthouse to shore on its western side.

Progressing slowly into the wind, we finally made it to a point where I felt we could turn into the harbor. I underestimated the wind's effect on the hull and had to steer hard to port just to go straight. I felt like our forward progress was measured in inches. With almost no visibility it was a miracle that we made it inside the harbor where the protection of the city breakwall calmed water conditions.

The storm still obscured my view and a lightning

strike was uppermost on my mind, but at least I wasn't struggling for control anymore. I held a south heading toward the river entrance, a three-hundred-foot wide target that I could barely see. Danny and Norm went to the bow, their eyes and ears helped guide us to safety.

After hours in the blinding storm, we made it to the river. I found a place to tie up on the western bank. As we secured the *Day Tripper*, the rain began to subside. Across a large empty lot, Danny spotted a little restaurant called the Harbor Café, I looked forward to a hot meal and a floor that wasn't going up and dow

In the cafe, Danny mulled over taking a Greyhound bus back to Cleveland. He'd pretty much had it with the nausea. The waitress overheard and said they had sea-sickness pills at the register, Danny bought a box of Dramamine and took a couple. When we left the cafe the storm had passed, leaving only light winds and rain. We resumed our trip, and Danny slept the whole way back.

Entering the Cleveland waterfront through the west breakwall cut, it was nice to finally be in home waters. The boat couldn't have performed better. An hour later, after securing the *Day Tripper* in its slip, I headed to my parents' house. I wanted to get out of my cold, damp, clothes and into a hot shower.

Note to self; gotta get me a rain poncho.

CHAPTER 11: HENRY'S BAD DAY

A month had passed since the burned boat hull had been hauled away. If anyone at the scrap yard realized that the bow-rail was removed, I think I'd have heard about the discrepancy by now. Kris lifted the rope tied to the sunken rail retrieving it from its hiding place, in the water beneath our slip.

The rail, black with soot and a substance that looked like charred melted rope, was otherwise in good shape. A thorough cleaning brought the stainless steel rail to its original condition. We carried it to its new location on the bow only to find that it was a few inches too wide on each side. Applying pressure from both sides, we could make the rear stanchions conform, but not the forward ones. We decided to re-stash the rail back under the boat and wait until we talked to Ivan; he'd know what to do.

A mechanical engineer, Ivan had the impressive ability to take one look at a difficult situation, then moments later, come up with a solution. Not only that but if special tools were needed, he probably had them. I called Ivan and explained the issue and, of course, he said, "Not a problem. I'll see you Saturday morning."

Ivan showed up with two come-along winches and a small welding torch. He easily finessed the width of the rail to match the curve of our bow. Once in place, we bolted the rail securely to the metal edge of the gunwale and we were finished. All before 9:00.

That night, Ivan returned to the marina for a poker game aboard Hank's boat. A couple of hours into the game, the phone rang, on the *Day Tripper* and Norm ran to answer it. The call was for Ivan. When he returned to Hank's boat, Ivan asked: "Guys, you want to learn how to butcher a steer tonight?"

A farmer who kept livestock for Ivan had called. His young steer, Henry, had wandered off the farm and onto the road where he tangled with an oncoming truck. Left with an injured leg, poor Henry needed to be dispatched as soon as possible.

We piled into Ivan's Mercedes and drove to a small farm fifty miles southeast of town. Ivan had an arrangement with a farmer named Frank to raise two steers. When it was time, he'd slaughter an animal to feed his large family.

Arriving at the farm near midnight, we were anxious to get to the task at hand. Frank, the farmer, invited us into his house where his wife Margaret poured us each a tall hot cup of coffee. She was a thin woman, friendly and dressed in overalls. Frank and her side by side reminded me of the *American Gothic* painting.

The farmhouse looked old and weathered, nothing looked in plumb and the plaster on the walls had been patched many times. Two exposed bulbs in an overhead porcelain fixture cast a pallid light in the large kitchen/dining room room combo.

A huge round table densely stacked with stuff that you'd expect to see in a cupboard, stood off to the left. Across the room, a big cast-iron wood-burning stove had a coffee pot warming on top and two cats lying comfortably on an open oven door. Shelves of preserved fruit covered the walls. A kitchen counter, a sink with a hand pump, and a dining table completed the room. If you wanted a drink of water, you had some pumping to do.

One new appliance, the refrigerator, stood out among 1940's motif. There were also two doorways, one closed, probably a bedroom. The other was open and led to a family room. It held three worn couches, a console color TV, and a dining table. Generations of family photos adorned the aged walls. It all appeared clean and mostly free of dust.

Frank and Margaret lived a simple life. They cooked and kept warm with wood from their trees. Their food was raised or grown by them and Frank sold milk to a local dairy. That's about as self-sufficient as people could be. He said his great-grandfather bought the forty-four acres and built the farm just after the Civil War.

Frank told us the injured bull was lying quietly in the corral. As he spoke he crumbled tobacco from a small white pouch into a rolling paper, then he cinched the bag shut holding its drawstring with his teeth. With the finesse of experienced fingers, he quickly folded himself a crude, hand-rolled cigarette.

I say folded because, it was nothing like the neat pencil thick joints that I was familiar with. Frank twisted together a working cigarette with a minimal effort in about five seconds.

Frank was short and wiry, his skin resembled the texture of a worn work glove. He was well spoken and lived comfortably within his environment.

Walking toward the barn, Ivan handed me a pistol and asked if I wanted to take care of the steer, I nodded. Ivan smeared a mud-spot in the middle of Henry the steer's head, "Put the bullet right there."

I had never killed anything bigger than a rat but, I knew the animal was suffering and it was destined for the dinner table. I distanced my thoughts from the killing and focused on a putting a humane end to the situation. Placing the muzzle against Ivan's mud spot was easier said than done, Henry kept moving, obscuring my aim.

Frank dropped some alfalfa in front of the steer, as he took a mouthful, I took the shot. He collapsed immediately as if someone had flipped a switch.

Soon the carcass hung in the barn doorway ready for processing. Kris, Norm and I removed the hide as Ivan did the gutting and butchering. He explained his methods as he skillfully broke-down the animal into four quarters of beef. Frank helped us prepare the hide, scraping, salting and rolling it into a bundle.

By dawn, we were on our way home with two-hundred-fifty pounds of quartered beef in the trunk. A few weeks later we were invited to Ivan's house for a prime rib dinner. Henry, it turned out, tasted delicious with a horseradish dipping sauce and mashed potatoes.

CHAPTER 12:
THE COMMANDO RAID

Bob, Perry, and Hank joined us for an afternoon fishing trip, hopefully, followed by a fish fry. With September approaching, perch were biting and most people caught their limit. We headed to our favorite spot, half-a-mile north of the east breakwall marker-light. An old shipwreck created a sheltered place for fish to hide, on an otherwise flat bottom.

By the second hour, we had over thirty perch and we were done fishing. I grabbed a book, sat in the shade, cracked open a beer, then heard everyone yelling excitedly. Popping up quickly, I saw Kris' rod bent so far over I thought it would snap. This wasn't a perch! Kris had hooked something capable of a fight. *What the hell could it be?*

Kris adjusted the drag and controlled the fish, the fight was on. It got pretty exciting, everyone stopped what they were doing as Kris moved around the deck following whatever the hell was on the hook. He had to be careful to keep the line from tangling on the prop or rudder.

After fifteen minutes, Kris brought the fish alongside the boat where we could see it. Holy shit! It was over two feet long.

He guided his catch to the stern where I netted it and brought it aboard. On the rear deck, I set down the net for Kris to take charge of it. In a second, the angry fish with a mouth full of scary teeth, was snapping and flipping all over the damn deck. Hank almost fell in the lake trying to stay away from the fish. It came aboard with more energy than anyone expected.

Kris threw a towel over the fish and tried to pin it down so he could remove the hook. Underestimating its strength, *the fish from hell* got its teeth on his fingers and there was blood all over the place.

I recognized it from the mural on the side wall of the bait shop, it was a northern pike, the number one trophy fish in Lake Erie.

Norm got a broom and I grabbed the boat hook. In the fracas that followed, the fish ended up flipping itself back into the lake. The hook and line were still attached to the pike, quick reflexes and sheer luck kept the fishing rod from going overboard. I cut the line and he was gone. No one could believe the havoc that fish created in ten seconds.

Kris' fingers were injured on both sides, a lot of small punctures and cuts, blood went everywhere.. Worried about infection, I handed him our military surplus first aid kit. As he poured a red liquid over his fingers, Kris lit up like a pinball machine on acid! Usually stoic and unemotional, Kris let out the loudest rendition of damn, shit, mother-fucker that I ever heard. It was Iodine.

* * *

When we started the engine, there was an odd noise. With the hatch open, I could see that the drive belt had come off the generator pulley. Upon closer inspection, a large chunk of the pulley was actually missing. We didn't have a functioning generator on the way home, but since the battery was fully charged, it wouldn't be an issue on such a short trip.

I hoped the pulley could be replaced with a standard automotive part, but it turned out it couldn't; its proprietary offset design, meant it had to be specially ordered. The *Chris Craft* dealer on the west side, where we usually bought engine parts, did not have the pulley in stock and it wasn't available from his distributor either. The counterman suggested we call other parts dealers around the country, or more likely, locate a used part.

We needed that pulley, so Norm and I went to a boat salvage yard just west of Gordon Park. We'd recently bought some hull parts from their yard including the mounting brackets for our new bow rail. The brackets came off an old hull, In fact, we removed them ourselves.

Grey Marine flathead engines like ours, were plentiful, and I hoped the part could be easily located. The old man in the office said he had a few boats in the yard with Greys. Handing me a small toolbox, he pointed us to the boatyard door.

Old hulls were everywhere, truly a place where boats go to die. Some were on their sides, a few in cradles, most were just propped against each other at various angles. We climbed through old boats for an hour before we hit pay dirt. Finally, in an old fishing boat, we found two mostly stripped, Grey Marine flatheads, but one of them had the pulley.

While I removed the part, Norm spotted a small dust-covered bright yellow box on a shelf. It caught his attention because of its good condition and metal reinforced corners. The box contained a brand new, Stromberg carburetor. I held it up to the Grey's intake manifold and it matched. I'd ask the counter man how much he wanted for the carb, it wouldn't hurt to have a spare, if the price was right.

If I'd had the proper wrench it would have shortened this chore to minutes, but removing the pulley with a crescent wrench, screwdriver, and pliers complicated the task. I smashed my knuckles a few times on the engine and cursed myself for not bringing my own toolbox.

In the office, I placed the pulley on the counter and the old man said "Fifty dollars." In my naïveté, I told him, that a brand new pulley only cost ten dollars, but they were out of stock. He laughed as did the fellows beside him, "Well, go buy a new one—or pay me fifty."

We paid the fifty dollars but I was so pissed I didn't even ask about the carburetor.

Back on the boat, Norm and I finished installing the pulley just as Kris arrived. He had a twelve-pack and a lid of weed. *Captain Frank's* was our destination, and we'd mellow-out along the way.

While talking about the events at the boatyard, I came up with an idea for a *commando-style* operation to swipe the carburetor from where we'd left it back on the shelf in the fishing boat. On the ride back to

Gordon Park we planned the *raid on the boatyard*.

After midnight, we borrowed one of Junior's aluminum fishing boats and headed to the salvage yard, twenty minutes away by water.

Kris let Norm and me off at the pier behind the boatyard. We climbed the ladder up to the darkened lot where the boats were stored. I spotted the old fishing boat with the boxed carburetor, maybe twenty yards away, the second hull in the center row.

Kris, in the *getaway boat* waited nearby for my flashlight signal; then he'd come in and pick us up at the ladder. At least that was the way we planned it.

Halfway to the old fishing boat, we were startled by the alarming sound of excited barking. Oh shit! Dogs! We turned and ran as fast as we could, reaching the pier with the dogs nearly upon us. There was no time for the ladder, we leaped, fully clothed off the pier, a fifteen-foot drop into the lake.

Swimming in a hooded sweatshirt and jeans took all of our energy. With great difficulty, Kris hauled us both aboard the little aluminum boat. With tears in his eyes from laughing so hard, he looked at us lying there exhausted and drenched. He said, "Nice raid, *commandos.*"

CHAPTER 13: THE BIG PARTY

Cleveland is split geographically by the Cuyahoga River. The lowlands of the mile-wide river valley near its mouth are known as *The Flats*. Once the domain of warehouses and factories, it was turning into a popular place for music, bars, and dining establishments. The gentrification of *The Flats* had begun.

Riverfront restaurants installed docks and patios catering to the welcomed boating trade. Nightclubs and bars popped up on the streets adjacent to the river. The area became trendy and customers were plentiful. On weekends, shortages of dock space, caused boats to tie together side by side, sometimes four deep. They came to join the revelry at a half dozen new establishments. Old empty warehouses turned into nightclubs like The Pirate's Cove, Flat Iron Cafe, Pickle Bills, and The Harbor Inn. Farther south, the river flowed past steel mills, refineries, and chemical manufacturers.

The Cuyahoga's claim to fame was being so polluted that it actually caught fire, *twice*. First in 1952 and again in 1969. The latter fire sparked the environmental movement that forced the city to take action to finally clean up the polluted river.

Near the Cuyahoga's mouth, a large vertical-lift railroad bridge opened to allow freighters and other vessels to navigate the river. When the bridge lowered small boats could make it underneath but the *Day Tripper* could not.

One evening Norm and I took our dates to dinner at one of the new riverfront restaurants. Everything went great and we all got along well. Afterwards, when we boarded the boat for the ride back to Gordon Park. The big iron bridge was lowered so we signaled the bridge-keeper with our horn. Waiting patiently got us nowhere; the bridge stayed down. Other boats, now waiting with us also blew their horns. One long blast followed by a short; the international whistle-code for raise the damn bridge!

Norm's date had to be home by midnight. We already had been waiting for an hour, with another hour's ride to Gordon Park still ahead. Making her curfew didn't look do-able and she became overly vocal blaming Norm, me, and my date. She was a cute girl, but her looks were overshadowed by her demeanor.

By eleven, the fifteen or more boats waiting for the bridge, all blasted our horns in unison. Within minutes, the bridge began to rise and we were finally on our way. I think the bridge tender fell asleep. The ride back to the marina was awkward.

Norm's date who had been so friendly earlier that evening, did her best to make us as uncomfortable as possible. She reiterated ad nauseam that her father would be furious. Norm tried to make the best of the situation, offering to explain the delay personally to her father. She remained insufferable and after spending those last few hours with her, Norm was more than happy to never see her again, and for that matter, so was I.

* * *

On Friday, the start of the long Labor Day weekend, Bob, three girls and Perry joined us for a day on the lake. We dropped anchor at our favorite fishing spot and I noticed there were more pleasure craft on the water than usual. Blue skies, calm waters, and sunshine brought the people out. Soon, the good days for boating would be few and far between as colder weather approached.

Perry got his line in the water first, immediately catching a fish. He started pulling in yellow perch, one after the other. Soon, with five of us fishing, we were landing perch as fast as we could re-bait our hooks.

I've done a lot of fishing, but never with these results. Between us, we caught a hundred and fifty perch, only stopping because we reached the legal limit. Our haul filled a large cooler and two big buckets, making them almost too heavy to lift. Only one thing to do: a Labor Day fish-fry on Sunday!

Junior gave us the okay, and we started making calls. We even invited our parents. My mom and dad had never even seen the *Day Tripper*.

We put the event together in just one day. Junior loaned us a commercial deep fryer and Hank came up with a couple of boxes of chicken legs and potatoes. Others in the marina volunteered side dishes or pitched in money for supplies. Junior and Della even provided free ice cream bars.

On party day, our parents came early so we could take them for a boat ride before everything got started. Although the three of us had been friends for years, our parents had never met. This would be the day.

My mother hadn't been on a boat since she'd arrived from Russia in 1921. She wasn't a boat person, but once the parents met and the socializing began, she thoroughly enjoyed her new experience.

My parents, Al and Iris, Norm's parents, Stan and Helen, and Kris' mom, Eleanor, all had a fun time on the boat. I don't think any of them thought that it would be so nice. I hoped they all left with a better understanding of why we enjoyed boating so much.

It took about two hours to cruise past downtown and back. The parents took turns steering the boat, including my mom. She took the last and longest turn at the wheel, guiding the boat into Gordon Park where I took over for docking.

Since I was thirteen, I had worked at my father's printed sportswear business. It seemed all of the time we spent together was work-related. I appreciated this rare opportunity to interact with my parents in a fun way. It was nice to go a couple hours without thinking, or talking, about *the shop*.

The party had just gotten started, but our parents declined to stay—this wasn't their thing. As night fell, we had an unexpected bonus, when three of Perry's friends, who had a garage-band, showed up and played rock-n-roll through the night.

As parties go, this one has remained one of the best in my memory. In all, about seventy people attended. Years later, Junior recalled it as the biggest bash ever held at Gordon Park.

I had an unforgettable time with my parents that day. They were both impressed with how nice the boat looked and how much fun they'd had. I felt proud, in fact, when I think of good times that I'd had with my parents, that day always comes to mind.

I made plans to take my father fishing, something he said he hadn't done in twenty years. But those plans got put off and never fulfilled. If I could go back and change things, Dad and I would have gone fishing.

* * *

After Labor Day, fall weather signaled the end of the boating season. As the days got colder, fewer boats remained in the marina. We helped Junior remove his fleet of aluminum fishing boats, then, the *Day Tripper* sat alone; we were the last to leave Gordon Park.

In early November two-inches of snow fell the day we headed for our winter dry-dock at the Edgewater Yacht Club. The boat would be hauled out and set on a cradle for the next six months. It had been one hell of a year, filled with unexpected situations and new friends.

I watched with mixed emotions as the large boat-crane removed the *Day Tripper* from the water. The boat had been the focus of our lives for the last ten months, I knew I would miss it.

The following weekend, we prepared the hull and engine for winter. Three tightly secured tarps covered the boat. On the lakefront, the winters are brutal.

* * *

The summer of 1968 brought many new experiences into my life. Things were changing fast and throughout the country, it would also be known forever as *The Summer of Love*.

In San Francisco, as many as 100,000 people converged on the Haight-Ashbury neighborhood initiating a major cultural and political shift. Hippies gathered in large cities across the country, including Cleveland. We protested the Vietnam War, smoked pot, had long hair, earrings, and flashed peace signs. Life was good in a way that may never be possible again.

CHAPTER 14: THE ROAD TO MIAMI

After living aboard the boat and having a taste of independence, the time had come for me to move out of my parent's home. Norm and Kris felt the same, so we rented a place together in the eastern suburb of Euclid. It was an older apartment, big by today's standards, with three bedrooms, a full kitchen, one bathroom and a twenty-foot-long living room.

Boredom and winter weather caused us to set up an indoor shooting range right in our apartment. I modified .22 caliber ammunition, making special indoor rounds that were quiet, safe, and accurate.

Using pliers, I removed the lead bullets from their cartridge cases, dumped-out the gunpowder, and pressed the empty case through a quarter-inch slab of paraffin wax. The result, an easy to make, low powered wax bullet. Sufficient propulsion came from the rim fire primer alone.

The noise from the shot was softer than a clap. Twenty-feet away, the wax bullet accurately marked the shot on a target. There was never a noise complaint from any neighbor.

One evening, Norm and I were practicing our shooting skills in the living room. We prepared about fifty special rounds, pulling the lead bullets and dumping the gunpowder into an ashtray.

By the time Kris got home, it was after eleven and the apartment was dark. Norm turned in earlier and was already asleep in his room at the far end of the hall. I was in my bedroom listening to the radio through a pillow-speaker.

I watched the apartment brighten momentarily as Kris grabbed something from the refrigerator. I heard his footsteps as he past my open door, entered his room and got into bed. As his custom, he lit his last cigarette of the day lying on his back staring at the ceiling. Minutes later he crushed the butt into the ashtray balanced on his belly.

Unknown to anyone, it was the same ashtray that I had filled with gunpowder earlier that evening. I'd forgotten to empty it and left it on the kitchen counter. Kris' room lit up like an orange flashbulb as he jumped out of bed yelling, "What the fuck! What the fuck!"

I sprang up, immediately realizing that I had forgotten to dump out the gunpowder. We were all up now, standing in the hallway. Kris was upset of course, and there was a burned dark circle with a white center right in the middle of his t-shirt. Fortunately, he wasn't injured, but the hair on his hand and arm were singed.

Once I explained that it wasn't a joke, Kris calmed down. Over the years we've gotten a lot of laughs out of the gunpowder incident. Not that evening, but over the years.

* * *

On Sunday, December 22nd we came up with the idea to drive to Miami Beach leaving the bad weather behind. Not having to be back at work until January 2nd, there was plenty of time.

Kris had purchased a new 1968 Simca sedan, a boxy little French car slightly larger than a Volkswagen Beetle. Its comfortable interior and good gas mileage made it a great choice for the thirteen-hundred-mile drive. Non-stop, we could make it to Miami in twenty-two hours. We'd stayed up that long before, many times. The drive should be a piece of cake.

The next day I picked up a set of auto club maps called *TripTiks*. We were ready to go. The maps contained fold-out inserts, and they were important. The inserts contained detailed instructions through the detours along the main route I-75. The highway was under construction in Kentucky and Tennessee where we'd have to divert to mountain roads for a couple of hours.

Leaving Cleveland late Monday night would assure we'd drive the mountain detours during the daylight. The plan was to be in Miami the following evening where we'd find a motel, get a full night's sleep and start our vacation, well rested, on Christmas day. Between us, we had almost $600.

In Kentucky, our first detour took us on a winding two-lane road that passed small towns, farms, and roadside attractions. Every curve in the road brought another interesting vision of life in rural Appalachia. I felt like we had transported into the past. Cars on the road were from the fifties, and people were riding horses. In one town I saw four young boys riding bareback on the same horse.

Colorful handmade quilts were displayed for sale on clotheslines in front yards. Signs along the road touted sorghum ham, sorghum bread, sorghum this and sorghum that. *It got me wondering, what the hell is sorghum?*

Then one sign that caught my attention read: "Last chance for a home-cooked meal before the Interstate." We couldn't pass on that offer; after all, it sounded a lot tastier than our breakfast at Howard Johnson's.

The little family restaurant did a brisk business. There was that word again on the menu, *sorghum*. I later learned that it was a form of molasses, it enhanced food with a sweet flavor.

Kris ordered a sorghum ham sandwich, Norm sorghum pancakes, and I went with bacon and eggs with grits. I'd never had the opportunity to try grits before, they were not offered on Cleveland menus. Lunch was delicious, but the grits were too bland. I've enjoyed them since, but not that day.

Rejoining the Interstate, we made our way through a series of construction zones and shorter diversions. In Tennessee, the last detour put us on a winding two-lane mountain road. The earlier scenery of farms, meadows, and gently rolling hills gave way to thick pine forests with sheer drop-offs along the side of the roads, some places had no guardrails.

An hour later, after winding through a never ending series of turns, an acrid smell filled the car. There was also a loud grinding noise. Kris pulled off the roadway to investigate. It turned out to be a total failure of the front right wheel bearing. The smell came from burned, smoking wheel bearing grease. We were disabled deep in the Tennessee woods.

Up ahead to the right, a dirt driveway, dusted by recent snowfall, led up a hill to a small cottage. Smoke rose from the chimney, so Kris and I headed over, hoping we could call *AAA* road service.

A frail woman of about thirty cracked open the door just enough to see us. I didn't blame her for caution; I doubt they got many long-haired hippie-type, walk-up visitors. Kris explained that our car broke down, and asked if she had a phone we could use. She did, but asked us to wait on the porch; she'd make the call for us. I handed her my *AAA* information envelope, and off she went.

Through the front window, we could see an older man sitting in a comfortable looking recliner. A scraggly, dried, Christmas tree stood against the far wall, wrapped presents at its base. It seemed odd to see a tree in such poor condition when the woods around us were filled with lush pines.

Returning, the woman let us know that a tow truck would be sent from Knoxville, fifty miles to the south. I asked where we were and she told me Habersham, Tennessee.

Kris gave her some money to cover the long distance call. Back at the car Norm was already snoozing. Kris and I took the opportunity to get some shut-eye ourselves, while we waited for rescue.

A couple of hours later the tow truck driver startled us awake by slapping hard on the windshield. For some reason, he seemed to be in a nasty mood. *Maybe he didn't want to be working on Christmas eve.*

The driver, short, thin with a full beard and a receding hairline immediately started to hook the Simca to the tow truck. Once he lifted the front end off the ground, I could see he mistakenly connected one of his tow hooks to the steering linkage. I pointed out his error and he gave me a long, glaring, nasty look.

"I've been towing for twenty years and I don't need your damn help hooking up a car," he snapped.

Lowering the car, he reattached the hook and sarcastically asked if he'd done it right that time. Norm went to climb into the warm cab of the tow truck. He was stopped by the tow truck driver who yelled, "Shut the damn door! You guys have to ride in the piece-of-shit Jap car."

Actually it was French.

The ride to Knoxville, with us in the Simca swinging wildly off the back of the tow-truck was flat-out frightening, and likely illegal. The crazy asshole driver drove too fast, which caused the us to veer dangerously wide around the twisting mountain roads. Kris blasted his horn repeatedly, but the driver ignored us. Finally, out of the mountains and back on the Interstate, we could stop holding our breath at each curve.

Reaching Knoxville after dark, The tow-truck driver unhooked us in a warehouse district in front of a closed *AAA* approved repair shop on Christmas Eve.

When I signed the paperwork, instead of my signature, I wrote *Fire this driver!* Then I wrote my phone number. The driver didn't even look at the form and no one ever called.

To our dismay, a sign on the repair shop's door read: *Happy Holidays, Closed until January 2nd.*

"Shit."

Looking around, the only open business on the block was a cab company depot/garage across the street. While walking over, snow began to fall.

The taxi company occupied a large brick building. Inside, cabs were parked in rows along the walls. One taxi was raised on a service lift and another, hood removed, needed an engine. In a windowed central office, a woman dispatcher, wearing an operator-style headset idly watched a portable television.

A group of five men stood together talking in the warm air blast below an overhead gas heater. We approached, introduced ourselves, and explained our plight. One man, who identified himself as the garage manager, talked through a scarf wrapped around his face saying, "You're welcome to use any tools or equipment in the garage. Help yourselves to coffee and donuts in the break room."

Dinner that night was three maple glazed donuts. It hit the spot.

Until I saw the closed sign on the auto repair shop's door, I hadn't considered fixing the car myself. Now it looked like that would be the only way to salvage this vacation.

My only experience with wheel bearings was repacking grease into the ones on my first car, a '56 Pontiac. Hopefully, this would be a similar job.

Rolling a floor jack out to the street, I lifted the front of the car and removed the brake drum from the axle. I noticed that a small broken section of the wheel bearing, a little nugget the size of a pea, had welded itself, by friction, firmly to the axle. This would be a more complicated job than I had anticipated.

The cab company mechanic came out, took a look and said, "You're going to have to replace the entire axle assembly, it's all one part."

My heart sank. It *sure-as-hell* wouldn't be an off-the-shelf item and the closest Simca dealer would likely be back in Cleveland. It seemed we were screwed and our vacation was over before it started. I envisioned the Simca being towed all the way back to Cleveland.

Staring at the damaged axle, I wondered if there was a way to fix it. No matter what, the spindle/axle assembly had to come off the car. Even though I had no experience with suspension and steering, I figured if I could remove it, I could probably put it back together. If this vacation could be salvaged, I knew We'd better get started.

Out on the snow-covered street, I studied the complexity of removing the damaged part without altering the important steering geometry. I glanced at Kris with an indecisive look.

"Go for it," He said.

Norm held the flashlight and kept track of the parts. He made detailed sketches showing the location of each nut, washer, and bushing.

Kris and I disassembled the front suspension and removed the spindle. Aside from the cold working conditions, the job went reasonably well. The small blob of metal welded to the axle needed to be removed by grinding and hand filing.

We took turns filing away at the unwanted lump of hardened steel. Progress was slow, but we finally removed it. Aside from a few pits in the metal, the damaged axle looked almost as good as new. The wheel bearing still had to be replaced, but no sense worrying about that until morning. We were cold, wet, and exhausted, and in need of a good night's sleep.

Kris and I walked into the manager's office to

thank him for his assistance and ask if there was a motel nearby. He turned toward us, the scarf, earlier covering his face, now lay loose around his neck. *He didn't have a nose!*

There was a triangular opening, but no nose. As he talked he constantly dabbed at the opening with a handkerchief. Not wanting to be impolite, and never before finding myself in this type of a situation, I tried my best to act normal.

The manager introduced himself as Ed and inquired how things went with the repair. We told him except for the bearing and re-assembly, we were happy with what we'd done so far.

Ed glanced at the wall clock, it was five minutes past midnight and now Christmas day. Taking a bottle from a drawer, he gestured toward the cup dispenser tube on the side of the water cooler. "Will you join me for a shot of Christmas shine?" he asked.

I didn't exactly catch the 'shine' part when he said it. But, not to be ill-mannered, we extended our paper cups and Ed poured. "Bottoms up," he said.

The drink's alcohol content literally took my breath away and puckered my face—no doubt the most potent thing I had ever swallowed. It burned all the way down, and then it burned some more. Ed got a big kick out of our reaction. With a big smile on his odd face he said in a heavy southern accent, "That's

Tennessee moonshine, boys."

Whatever caused the loss of his nose will always be a mystery to us, but on Christmas of 1968, five hundred miles from home, we needed a friend, and we found one in Ed.

He drove us to the *Admiral Benbow Inn* a few blocks away. At this point, except for a short nap, we'd been up for damn-near forty hours.

As he dropped us off, Ed said, "Good luck guys, I hope you're back on your way to Florida soon."

Christmas morning, I started making calls trying to find an open auto-parts store, but, of course, there were none. The motel manager suggested we call the local newspaper and ask if they knew of a parts store that might be open on Christmas. I'll admit it. I didn't think it sounded promising, but what the hell, there weren't a lot of options.

I called the newspaper office and by sheer luck, talked to someone that thought he could help. He had an uncle who owned an auto parts distribution company on the outskirts of Knoxville. He'd make a call and get back to me.

A few minutes later the newspaper guy called back. His uncle would open the business for us and check if he had the proper bearing. I took down the address and we ran the five blocks to the cab garage.

Grabbing the broken bearing, spindle and brake drum, we jumped into a cab and headed to the parts distributor fifteen miles out of town.

Our driver pulled up to a three-story brick home. Next to it, stood a large warehouse building with a nondescript name painted on the side.

An older gentleman came out of the house and greeted us with a smile and a handshake. He told us his they call him *Ole Red*. We exchanged holiday greetings and followed him into the warehouse. It turned out his company supplied auto parts to most of the retailers in Tennessee.

I laid our broken parts on the counter and he took measurements. After thumbing through a stack of manuals, he walked into the back without saying a word. I have to admit, at that point, I had little hope he would find a Simca wheel bearing.

A few minutes later he reappeared holding two small boxes. It seemed our broken wheel bearing matched the one used on millions of Volkswagen Bugs.

"Anything else?" he asked.

"I'll take a can of wheel bearing grease."

Ole Red placed the items in a paper sack and

handed it to me.

"How much?" I asked.

With a broad smile, he said: "Merry Christmas, it's on the house—just send me a postcard from Miami Beach."

We thanked *Ole Red*, also wishing him a Merry Christmas. Returning to our cab, we headed back to the garage. It was emotionally uplifting that so many people extended themselves to help three strangers in our time of need.

At the garage, we put everything back together and by noon we were on the road again.

With the exception of the crazy tow-truck driver, the generosity and help we received from everyone we'd met in Knoxville will not be forgotten. God bless them all. With eight-hundred miles to go, our vacation was back-on.

I drove all the way to Macon, Georgia while Kris and Norm caught up on sleep. Then I moved into the back seat and they took over driving. "Wake me when you see a Palm tree," I said.

CHAPTER 15: THE TROPICS

There were no further mechanical problems on the Florida trip. Now, almost at the end of our long drive, time seemed to slow as my excitement grew. Passing exit signs for West Palm Beach, Boca Raton, and Ft. Lauderdale heightened my anticipation. Finally, after 1,300 miles, the sign above the interstate read: *Arthur Godfrey Causeway, Miami Beach, Next Left.*

The causeway took us across Biscayne Bay to the man-made barrier island that *is* Miami Beach. I thought about the contrast in climate between here and back home. In Cleveland, people were freezing, driving through dirty slush and snow. Here it was eighty degrees at midnight, with a floral fragrance in the air.

Without a pre-made reservation, we were heading to the one and only address that I knew in Miami Beach, the *Shepley Hotel*, 1340 Collins.

* * *

Before I was born, my family had a short history in Miami Beach. For a few years, my parents, along with my aunt and uncle, owned a hotel right in the center of Old Miami Beach. We decided to check the hotel out and, hopefully, stay there, at least for the first night.

The Causeway took us to Collins Avenue where we turned south. I counted down the addresses until we finally reached 1340. There it stood, the *Shepley* looking exactly like the old postcard in the family album.

All my life, I'd heard about the *hotel in Florida*. Now as I stood right in front of it, I thought about an old photo that I remembered. in the picture, my mother, father, grandmother, and sister all sat right there, on those three steps. They all wore tropical white linen, my dad with a Panama hat.

In the mid-forties My parents along with my aunt and uncle bought the Miami Beach hotel. They left cold weather behind to live in the tropics. Shit happened and I later learned their deepest regret had been selling the hotel in 1947 and moving back to Cleveland. It was their dream, their plan for the future, a once-in-a-lifetime opportunity, lost before it really began.

The story, I'd heard about my family leaving Florida, blamed my aunt, she wasn't able to deal with separation from her family and friends. My mother said that Aunt Sophie would spend days crying and moping around. It made everyone miserable, including the hotel guests. High-strung and accustomed to getting her own way, she invited her friends and relatives to come stay at the hotel. Without charge!

With only twenty-five guest rooms available, every dollar was needed to pay the mortgage and operating expenses. With rooms constantly given away, the profits weren't there. To avoid family arguments they sold the hotel and returned to Cleveland. I'm not really sure if I've got the story right, nobody really wanted to talk about it.

* * *

This section of Miami Beach was a collection of small art-deco hotels mixed with mom and pop shops. It turned out that most of the hotel rooms in this area had been repurposed into studio apartments for retired seniors. The *Shepley* was no different and didn't have rooms available.

That first night, we needed a place to stay and it wasn't going to be in this area. Luckily, a group of people we'd met on the street knew the town and clued us in. They directed us to Sunny Isles, five miles up the coast, past 163rd street. They said, "That's the fun Miami Beach, this is a retirement village."

The drive north took us past big well-known hotels, like the Diplomat, Sands, Algiers, and the jewel of Miami, the Fontainebleau. Their marquees lit up in bright lights, with names like Dean Martin, Jackie Gleason, Paul Anka, Bobby Darin, and Frankie Avalon. The streets were filled with tourists, even late at night.

As we passed the 163rd Street Causeway, we could see that this is where the younger crowd congregated. At 1AM, the streets were buzzing with tourists. To our right on the beach side, stood the Castaways Hotel, followed by the Newport and the Sahara. The big hotels were on the ocean side of Collins Avenue, also known as A1A, and smaller motels lined the other side.

Being the height of the tourist season, motel after motel displayed "no vacancy" signs. Finally, we found a small Spanish style place that just had a no-show guest. The clerk said he'd just shut-off the no vacancy sign, turned around and we pulled in. The room, at twenty dollars a night, fit our budget just fine.

I was tired, but there was one thing I wanted to do before I went to sleep. Alone, I crossed Collins Avenue and walked towards the beach. Reaching into the warm waves lapping at the shoreline, I dipped my fingers into the salty ocean and tasted salt water for the first time, I was surprised how salty it actually tasted.

The next morning, we awoke to the sounds of progress; a pile driver hammered big cement pilings deep into the ground in the vacant lot next to our motel. The pounding felt like little tremors, one jolt every ten seconds. I guess that's why the room was so cheap. Ka-chunk, ka-chunk, ka-chunk! The construction went on from eight in the morning until three in the afternoon.

I easily overlooked the noise; this was Miami Beach, a paradise. Outside our motel room the fauna, flora, sunshine blue skies and whatever—looked like a tropical painting.

Brunch at Wolfe's Rascal House was delicious. I had the Mort Saul plate, a bagel with cream cheese and lox. The walls in Wolfie's were covered with autographed headshots of big-name stars, singers, and comedians. This was a popular spot. The waiter told us we just missed Art Carney, *yeah right.*

The streets were lined with palm trees, some with coconuts. Plants and blooming flowers were completely different from anything I'd seen in Ohio. Little lizards ran through the shrubbery, If you confronted some of them, they'd flair their orange frill and try to frighten you. Gotta give them credit, taking that last courageous stand, before turning and running.

As a kid, I bought a live lizard once at the circus for a dollar. Now I know where they got them all. They are literally everywhere.

Across the street, the ocean had a wide beach that went north and south as far as you could see. This was the tropics, and I was digging it. That first day we walked through the lobbies, and grounds of all the big hotels. We people-watched our way northward along the coast, checking everything out. To me, this was all new and exciting.

I'd never seen this kind of luxury. Rolls Royces, Bentleys, and foreign sports cars were commonplace. Beautiful young girls in bikinis stood on every corner.

Reaching the last big hotel, we switched from the street side to the beach side. Our walk back would be through the sand and the view from the beach side was fantastic.

Behind the Newport Hotel, I spotted Lou Rawls, the singer, standing at an outdoor bar cart. I approached and bought a pop while introducing myself.

"Big fan," I said, "Tobacco Road is one of my favorite albums."

"Why don't you come to the show tonight, here at the Newport?"

"Were going to the dog track. But, it was nice to have met you." *I just said to Lou fucking Rawls!*

We did indeed have dog track plans. Norm's Uncle Nate, who lived in Coconut Grove, an upscale suburb south of Miami, invited us to dinner at Flagler Dog Track.

Uncle Nate made his living by handicapping racing greyhounds. He published a daily tip-sheet that sold at Flagler and Hollywood Dog Tracks. He was a well-known, respected handicapper, his tip-sheets sold under the name Nick Carter's Picks.

Why not Uncle Nate's picks? Well, Uncle Nate explained it to us. He purchased the *Nick Carter's Picks* business ten years earlier, from a guy who bought it from a guy, who bought it from the original Nick Carter. The name was the whole deal!

When Uncle Nate retires, Nick Carter will no doubt, live on through its next owner.

Norm's uncle took us to dinner at the Flagler clubhouse. Then we placed some bets under the personal tutelage of Nick Carter himself.

We played quenelles, trifectas, perfectas, and exactas. My only previous betting experience was win, place, or show. I didn't know these types of bets even existed. That night we left the track almost two hundred dollars ahead!

Winning money at the dog track seemed so easy, that the next night we went back, without Uncle Nate, only to lose *all* of our previous winnings. There went my new dream plan of moving to Florida and living off my dog-track winnings. It seemed so easy the night before.

* * *

A group of girls in the motel room next-door, told us about a dance club up the street called *Thee Image*. They said, "You have to check it out."

They were going back to New Jersey that day, one of the girls said, "It's a ten dollar cover, but it includes three drink tickets. Well worth it."

Thee Image, built inside a converted bowling alley was spacious, psychedelic, and mind-blowing. Clubs in Cleveland were nothing at all like this. Black lights illuminated the room, smoke machines filled the dance floor with a knee-deep swirling mist. Strobe lights flashed, an oil/slide light-show simultaneously throbbed to the beat on four large screens. All of this stoked the excitement of the crowd.

On a central raised stage, the house band, *Blues Image*, played a loud set that included their big radio hit-single, *Ride Captain Ride*.

We had a lot of fun at the club and hooked up with a trio of Chicago girls, who hung with us for a while. We even listened to Paul Anka's live show at the Diplomat Hotel. Not having showroom tickets, we sat in the hotel's beach-side veranda where we could easily hear the music from the main floor.

The next morning we had breakfast with the girls before they left for the airport. As we parted company, one of them handed me a baggie containing some half-dried brownish twig-looking things. She laughed and said, "These are Magic Mushrooms, divide them all between you, you'll have a good time."

Although accustomed to smoking pot, our trio hadn't had the opportunity to try hallucinogenic mushrooms. Bob once told me that he'd tried them at a party and would definitely do them again.

I chopped up the Magic Mushrooms, and made three equal piles to add to our food at dinner. Norm and I had chili-dogs and Kris had an open-faced roast beef sandwich. If I had it to do over, I would have downed the 'shrooms without any chewing, to avoid the stale nasty taste.

After dinner, we crossed the street and sat down in the patio-bar behind the Castaways Hotel. I ordered a round of colas and we waited for the onset of our psychedelic experience. We didn't know what to expect.

By the time the waitress arrived with our drinks, I sensed a small change in the way I heard the background music. Jazz playing over the speakers sounded different. The richness of the instrumentals flowing into the melodies harmonized in an amazing way that seemed to include the lights in the room. *What the hell!*

Though the room was noisey, a saxophone solo sounded so clear it could have been played from the next table. Lost in the music, I didn't hear Kris calling my name.

"Lenny, Lenny! *You* got this round."

I looked at the server, who was *stunningly beautiful.* Red lips, green eyes, and blonde hair, Marilyn Monroe-ish.

"Three dollars, sir," she purred.

I gave her a five and said, "Keep it,"

I watched her exaggerated gait as she slowly sauntered off. Step by step, she looked like a goddamn movie star.

If I just hallucinated her good looks—I was good with it. To me at that time, she was the most beautiful girl I had ever seen.

The mushrooms had a mild and calming effect, although my sight, hearing, and tastes were exaggerated. Checking with the guys, they felt the same. A sip of cola startled my senses with its souped-up, exaggerated carbonated flavor, I actually heard the bubbles go snap, crackle, and pop, tickling the inside of my nose and almost bringing on a sneeze.

The vibrancy and sparkle of colors coming from every light source gave the room a richness of texture that couldn't be ignored. I knew I was *on mushrooms* and I just felt an all-over warm and friendly feeling.

Perhaps an hour since ingestion, music, lights, and taste were turned up way past ten. I felt damn good, there were no spins, no dizziness, or disorientation. The effects were ethereal and I felt clear-headed and relaxed.

Our patio table offered a great all-around view. We were outside, under the stars, seated between the Atlantic Ocean and a hundred, or so dinner guests.

On the beach, a bonfire roared, it's flames, sparks, and smoke captured my attention. The movements of the flickering inferno seemed to draw my gaze. This was incredible. I was moved to watch for what may have been ten-minutes—it was so peaceful.

I looked at Kris as he lit a cigarette, something seemed different but I couldn't pinpoint it. His mustache! I couldn't remember if Kris always had a mustache or did he just grow it. I've seen him nearly every day for the last year, and I didn't know the answer.

Kris, observing my puzzled expression, said, "What?"

"Did you just grow that?" I asked.

"Grow what?"

"The mustache."

Norm, hearing our exchange, had just taken a drink of his cola. He gasped and laughed mid-swallow, causing the soda to eject from his nostrils in a bubbly brown blast of foam! I jumped back from the table to keep from being sprayed.

Seeing that, Kris and I burst out laughing. We couldn't stop ourselves. The more we tried the more ridiculous we looked. I don't know how long it went on, seconds, minutes, who knew?

Then, we became aware that all the diners in the restaurant had stopped eating and were staring directly at us. It got dead-quiet for a second or two, and time seemed to stop for a moment, kind of a strange few seconds. Then, in the blink of an eye, everyone returned to what they were doing before our comedic interlude.

Struggling to compose ourselves, we tried to look normal. Not an easy task. I couldn't suppress the sight of the foam spraying from Norm's nose, and I nearly lost it again. I regained control, took a deep breath and looked at Kris. Kris looked at Norm. Norm looked at me, and bam! We went-off again, laughing like stoned idiots. However, being aware of our moronic display minutes earlier, we tried to kept the hilarity at an acceptable bar-room level.

Nature called, so I headed to the men's room. Tiled in a tropical motif, the room was beautiful. In place of your normal four or five wall-mounted urinals, there was a big, wide, trough-style receptacle tiled right into the wall and floor. Noticing another patron at the far end, I kept a respectful distance and relieved myself into the communal structure.

Focused on my shimmering urine stream, I watched as a flow of glittery piss, in prismatic colors hit the back urinal wall. The splashes separating into rivulets of yellow, orange and blue. Foolishly, I must have said, or done, something stupid. The other fellow, now finished, asked if I was okay?

"I'm good," I chuckled and snickered.

Back at the table, Kris and Norm were talking to the waitress and laughing it up. Then, as I sat facing the bar, I noticed the guy from the bathroom talking to the bartender and pointing our way. *This can't be good.*

"Guys, let's get outta here," I said.

Kris, enjoying his chat with the waitress, ignored my warning. I told Norm about the sparkly piss and the guy in the bathroom. He also saw him pointing and understood we needed to split, the sooner, the better.

Leading Kris out of the bar by his elbows we shuffled towards Collins Avenue where hopefully we'd blend-in with the circulating crowd. I was surrounded by people but still felt good. I talked and socialized my way along the main drag in front of the big hotels.

Out on the sidewalk, the lights of the hotel Christmas displays had more prominence, more glitter, they looked beautiful. How did I miss this sight the other day? In my heightened state of awareness, everything looked spectacular. The bright colored lights of hotels and traffic moved in cadence with the music in my head. Sure-footed and alert, I was having a great time. After an short time standing motionless, we moved on.

Approaching a group of girls on the street, my normal shyness was gone. I engaged in conversations without hesitation. I'm not sure if I made any sense or not, but I didn't care. It was fun and I charmed the ladies. I don't know how long we'd been talking when one of the girls led Kris to a nearby stand of palm trees. In their semi-isolation, they started kissing.

The rest of us talked for a while before buying a gallon of wine and moving our little group to the beach behind the hotel. *These are all good-looking girls, I can't believe how well the evening is going. These mushrooms are amazing!*

We walked through the hotel lobby, to the beach where music from a nearby wedding tent played loud and clear. The only thing that could make this night go better is me getting laid. At the time, it looked like a strong possibility.

A row of lounge chairs provided the perfect party spot. Kris broke out our two remaining joints. We kicked off our shoes, danced, sang, drank, smoked, rocked, and rolled, we were *tripping the light fantastic*. Whatever that meant, we were doing it.

I carried on long meaningful conversations with no idea what I was talking about. It was extraordinary. A few hours later, with full-on munchies, we found ourselves at an outdoor Mexican restaurant. Tacos, burritos, whatever the hell we ate, it tasted good! Not just good, but without a doubt, the best food I'd ever eaten.

I was buzzed on wine, stoned and still tripping on the *shrooms*. My memories of that evening were split into short disconnected vignettes. We were here; we were there. Somewhere, I held on to a brown stuffed three-foot alligator.

I don't remember where or when we parted company with the girls, but the next morning the three of us were back in our motel room. I awoke at six, fully dressed, on the couch.

Well, as far as I remembered, I didn't get laid, but I sure had a good time. I picked the *roaches* out of our ashtray and re-rolled them into what would later be a nasty tasting last-joint. I moved to my bed for couple more hours of sleep. I hoped we can find that taco shop again.

* * *

Eight days ago we were knee-deep in winter. Now, sitting at our motel pool in this tropical climate, I thought about the snow, sleet, and slush that waited for us back home. This had been an enlightening, fun trip, including our car trouble in Tennessee. Years from now, I have no doubt, my Christmas in Knoxville will be one that stands out in my memory. We interacted with good people who displayed amazing generosity. Hell! Even the asshole tow-truck driver left us with a funny story to tell.

I had some new experiences in Miami. I'd won and lost money at the greyhound track, seen the Shepley Hotel, and took a trip on psychedelic mushrooms. Not bad for my first real vacation without the involvement of my parents.

* * *

Pooling our money, we had under fifty-dollars, enough for gas home, a bunch of peanut butter and jelly sandwiches, and a couple dozen sodas for the long drive. I remembered to mail postcards to family, friends, and, of course, *Ole Red* in Tennessee.

We'd leave for home at midnight. The late departure put us through the mountain detours in Kentucky, and Tennessee during daylight.

With one last full day to work on our winter tans, we headed for the beach. Luckily, a volleyball game needed players, so we took off our shirts and joined the fun.

As evening approached, we drove to Biscayne Bay to check out the local marina culture. Walking up and down the docks. I was amazed to see the sheer volume of beautiful boats and modern functional marinas, many with grocery stores, bars and restaurants. We did see some interesting wooden double-ended trawlers, but I didn't see anything like the *Day Tripper*.

As we strolled from pier to pier, we talked with local boaters when we had the opportunity. Then we came upon an unexpected sight. A boat on the dock up ahead flew the familiar pennant of the Cleveland Yacht Club. I picked up my pace when I saw the flag. Sure enough, a big classic motor yacht had The Emerald Necklace Cleveland, Ohio on its transom.

On the bow, a man hosing down the deck had his back to us. To get his attention, I called out, "Ahoy! Ahoy, on the Emerald Necklace."

He turned and walked toward us, we introduced ourselves as fellow Clevelanders. I told him I recognized the pennant flying on his stern flagpole. Terry, the owner, invited us aboard and introduced us to his wife, Christine. She picked up a large pitcher of sangria and poured us three tall fruit-filled drinks. They were superb.

After he retired a few years earlier, Terry brought the *Emerald Necklace* down from Cleveland. He traveled the Erie Canal and the Intercoastal Waterway, a three-month journey. The Intercoastal is a continuous, navigable, inland waterway built and maintained by the government. It runs along inside the coast, from Boston to Brownsville Texas.

We got a full tour of the Emerald Necklace, a sixty-five-foot Matthews motor yacht. It had four bathrooms, five staterooms, and bunked an additional six people.

Terry and Christine asked us to join them for dinner. She'd already made a casserole. That sounded much better than PB&J sandwiches back at the motel. We accepted their invitation.

Time flew by and at ten o'clock, we thanked our new friends for their hospitality and headed back to our motel. Everything was ready to pack into the Simca and go. By eleven, we were headed north on I-95. Thirteen-hundred miles to go.

Kris and Norm would share the driving to Georgia while I slept in the back seat. Then, I'd take over driving all the way to Knoxville while they slept. We'd all be awake for the last leg to Cleveland. The car ran flawlessly. Rain slowed us down a bit and it took us over twenty-four hours to make it to Cincinnati. With only a little over two-hundred-fifty miles to go, a northeastern snow storm hit us head-on.

White-out conditions forced all northbound traffic on Interstate 71 into a large truck stop. Inside, other stranded travelers had already staked out places on the floor. Hundreds of cars and trucks were stranded. The overwhelmed restaurant quickly ran out of food. We set up a makeshift couch along the wall with our suitcases and a duffel bag. At least it was warm in the building and we had a place to sleep. Our rations were down to ten sodas and nine sandwiches.

A family with two young kids *camped* on the floor next to us. They'd arrived late, after the food ran out, and hadn't eaten since lunch. Norm gave them six of our remaining sandwiches and some sodas. That left three for us in the morning and that was all we needed.

The storm let up after midnight. At three in the morning, they announced that vehicles with tire-chains could get back on the highway. By daybreak, the interstate had opened to all traffic.

In the morning, the truck-stop offered free coffee and donuts as a courtesy to the stranded, hungry, travelers. We each grabbed a couple extra donuts for the road.

The Cincinnati-to-Cleveland drive would normally take four-hours. That day, poor road conditions stretched it to over twelve. In Mansfield, with an almost empty gas tank and eighty miles to go, we spent the last of our money, under two dollars, on gas. This vacation worked out down to the exact last cent.

Finally, pulling into Kris' parking space behind our apartment building; two feet of fresh snow lay on the ground and it was 28 degrees. There's a certain beauty to freshly fallen snow, but for me, I enjoy it more on a postcard than in-person.

CHAPTER 16:
OUR SECOND YEAR

In early April of 1969, we removed the winter tarps and got to work preparing the *Day Tripper* for its return to the water. The boat looked good; it handled winter storage well. I drained antifreeze from the engine block, changed the oil, points, condenser and spark plugs. The engine started and ran smoothly after a short warm-up. With the mechanicals done, scraping, sanding, and painting were all that needed to be done.

At a large hardware store named *Uncle Bill's*, I purchased paint for the hull, deck, and interior. I also picked up one gallon of an expensive special anti-fouling coating for the bottom of the hull. The copper-based paint prevented vegetation from growing below the waterline.

An attractive young paint clerk helped me with my selections. Her name was Mollie. She had shoulder-length dark-brown hair flipped at her shoulders and ratted high on top, a popular style of the day. Mollie had an exceptional smile and pretty green eyes, not only that, but she was built like a *brick shithouse*.

I told her I wanted to get to know her, take her to a movie or something. She said she had a boyfriend. I wasn't surprised, she was gorgeous. Anyway, I gave her one of our newly acquired *Day Tripper* business cards. I told her to call me if she ever wanted to go for a ride on my yacht. I don't usually refer to the boat as a yacht, but I was going for maximum effect.

"Yacht, how big is your yacht?" she asked sarcastically.

.

"Thirty-five feet long. Longer than this paint aisle," I stated proudly.

She left to take care of another paint customer. As I watched her walk away, she lifted my card into the air and I thought she said something about a rain-check.

Rain-check? Did she say rain-check? I had a feeling I'd see Mollie again.

* * *

April of 1969 brought rain, rain, and more rain. We needed a dry day to complete the paint job, but the weather wouldn't cooperate. With a week to go before our scheduled Saturday launch, only a primer coat had been applied to the hull.

On Wednesday, our luck changed, clear skies were in the forecast. Thursday, we all played hooky from work and painted from sunrise to sundown. We rolled, brushed, and trimmed every exterior surface on the boat, it looked fantastic. Friday, the paint dried in

144

the sunshine.

On launch day, we arrived at the storage yard before eight. Driving down the rows of stored boats we were met head-on by a *Travel-Lift* coming our way with the *Day Tripper* already hanging in its slings. They were ahead of schedule.

Once launched, we checked for leaks, adjusted the stuffing box, and warmed up the engine; all systems were go. With Norm and I running the boat and Kris in his car, we'd meet at Gordon Park in about ninety minutes.

Not prepared for the chill created by the wind off the forty-seven-degree lake, our exposed skin quickly felt painfully cold. The blankets, towels, and extra clothing that we normally carried aboard were at home waiting to be laundered. Norm and I swapped positions between the cabin and the wheel every five minutes to deal with the numbing cold on our fingers and faces. With no heat in the cabin, at least we got relief from the wind.

Turning into Gordon Park, we saw Kris standing at the end of our pier waving his arms over his head. He indicated we should dock in Hank's empty slip instead of ours. Kris helped with the lines, jumped aboard, went to the rail and said, "Take a look at this shit."

He pointed toward our slip where through the rippling surface distortion, I could barely make out a solid yellow shape. I looked at Kris as he blurted out, "It's a goddamn sunken boat!"

We went to the bait shop, found Junior and told him about the problem. He was as surprised as we were. Someone, we surmised, abandoned the boat before the lake froze. After the thaw, the ice-damaged and broken hull leaked and the boat sank in place.

Until he figured out how to remove the sunken boat, Junior offered us another slip, but it was on the other side of the marina. We weren't interested; instead, I told Junior that we'd take care of the problem ourselves. At the time, I was thinking dynamite.

Ivan immediately nixed my idea of blowing the boat up. Instead he offered his help and equipment, explaining how we could re-float the cruiser using fifty-five-gallon drums. We'd place them along side the hull, two at the bow, two at the stern, and one attached to the engine offsetting its extra weight. We'd connect them together with ropes forming a makeshift lifting cradle. Then, using an air compressor and two long hoses, we would displace the water in the sunken drums with air until the boat became buoyant.

Bob and I volunteered for the underwater work, while Norm, Kris, Perry, and Ivan helped from the pier.

Ivan had three complete scuba rigs; I wore his single tank outfit and Bob, being bigger, used Ivan's heavier twin tank setup. A third tank was available for me to swap-out when needed. We rented two wetsuits, hoods, gloves, and booties, the forty-seven-degree water meant we needed to be fully protected from the cold. Our limited diving experience didn't cause any concern since we'd be working at a depth of only fifteen feet.

My first experience putting on a slightly smallish wetsuit proved to be difficult. The suit, made of quarter inch neoprene fit like a tight surgeons glove. I practically had to be a contortionist to put it on, overheating myself in the process. Jumping into the water to cool off helped. The water felt shockingly cold for four long seconds before the layer of water between me and the suit stabilized, then it was comfortable.

Underwater visibility was poor; we could see maybe six-feet. Once we started stirring things up on the bottom, visibility dropped to even less.

Bob was able to lift the bow off the bottom high enough for me to weave a couple of ropes back and forth connecting the two forward drums in a makeshift sling. Getting the ropes under the stern would be a lot more difficult due to the weight of the engine. Our solution; offset the motor's weight with a single drum tied directly to the engine's lifting ring. After filling it with air, the drum's added buoyancy allowed Bob, using an eight-foot pipe as a lever, to lift the stern high enough for me to swim under it with the ropes.

As I pulled the last rope under the boat I felt a whoosh of water push past me as the hull came down across the back of my legs pinning me to the mucky bottom. *Oh my God, what the hell just happened!* I immediately thought the drum attached to the engine must have come loose. *Yeah, that had to be what happened!*

Unknown to me, the buoyancy drum hadn't come loose, Bob had run out of air. Normally air flows freely through the scuba regulator mouthpiece, but as the tank empties, it becomes harder to draw a breath. Bob pulled on the rod that engaged the reserve air supply only to find that it was mistakenly left in the reserve position! There would be no additional air from the tank.

Bob, out of breath and thinking I'd already had time to clear the hull, let go of the transom and swam to the surface. When he saw I didn't come up, he had an ominous feeling. Quickly grabbing the almost empty spare tank that I had switched-out an hour earlier, he jumped back into the water to find me. The empty tank contained only a few minutes of breathable air
.

Meanwhile, pinned under the hull, I started freaking-out as I struggled to free myself, but my calves were stuck in the muddy bottom. *Why wasn't Bob helping me? Surely everyone must have seen the*

buoyancy drum come shooting up out of the water.
Where's Bob? Then, when it seemed things couldn't
get worse—a new issue arose.

I became aware that it took more effort to draw in
a breath! *My tank was running low! I* engaged the
reserve lever, and that helped a little, but I thought,
*they'll have to re-sink the drum, tie it back to the
engine and then refill it with air! That would take an
hour, I had maybe ten minutes of air left!*

My only chance was to put everything I had into
the most powerful push, squirm, and squiggle that I
could muster. I prayed I'd be able to free myself. I took
three deep breaths to oxygenate my blood gaining as
much strength as possible. Then I went for it. I gave it
my best effort, but I couldn't get out from under that
hull.

"Shit, fuck, fuck!" I hollered to myself.

Then, I felt a tug on my tank and turned my head
to see Bob, we were mask to mask. He saw the hull on
my legs, gave me the OK hand signal, and he
disappeared. What the hell, where did he go? Why
wasn't he helping me get loose? I didn't tell him I was
on reserve. Where did he go? I asked myself in panic.
Then, I felt the weight of the hull lift slightly and I got
my legs out as fast as I could.

My fins came off in the struggle and without them, I couldn't generate enough thrust to swim to the surface in this heavy gear. Then I remembered my weight belt! I lifted the quick-release closure and the belt fell away. With every last bit of strength left in me, I swam for the surface. Finally, in fresh air, I gasped and let out a feeble, "Help."

A hand reached down and took hold of my shoulder strap. Everyone tried to lift me onto the pier, but I was too heavy wearing the scuba gear. Kris, with all his clothes on, jumped into the cold lake and got me out of the tank harness. The next thing I knew I was face down on the pier, exhausted and overheated, but thankfully alive.

Bob rolled me over, pulled off my hood and unzipped the wetsuit to my waist. I laid there motionless, not injured, just completely, utterly, exhausted. A few minutes later, Norm handed me a cold root beer; it hit the spot.

Ivan and Kris left with the empty tanks. They detoured to Ivan's house where Kris got into some dry clothes. When they returned with the filled tanks, we were anxious to get back to raising the sunken boat. With the lifting cradle nearly finished, I hoped to complete the job that day.

It took another refill of the tanks, but everything was finally rigged and secured to the hull. Using two air compressors with twenty-five-foot hoses, we began to fill the drums with air. By late afternoon, the cruiser floated at the surface, its deck just below water level.

With five of us pulling lines attached to the lifting harness, we maneuvered the boat bow-first into one of the public boat launching ramps. Then, after removing

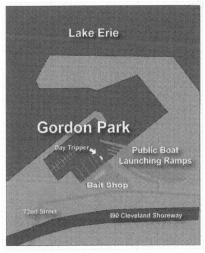

our lifting apparatus, the bow rested at the water's edge.

Perry borrowed a large tow truck from his father who owned a scrap metal business, the big truck seemed suitable for the task at hand.

He wrapped a long steel tow cable twice around the cruiser and back to the truck. Inch-by-inch he dragged the waterlogged hull up the ramp. Once the transom was exposed, I chopped a hole in the stern and it drained as Perry continued dragging the boat.

The truck pulled so hard, that at times, its front wheels came three-feet off the ground.

Meanwhile, a large crowd had gathered at the municipal ramps. It wasn't every day that you saw a bucking bronco tow-truck use brute-force to drag a sunken cabin cruiser out of the lake. A couple hours later the salvaged twenty-five-foot boat rested on its side, near the marina fence.

The next morning Perry began the tedious process of removing every brass screw from the drying hull. It took him three days to extract them all. When finished, the hull was reduced to a loose pile of mostly wood. Perry, who knew the value of scrap brass, ended up making almost two hundred dollars from the screws and fittings.

Over the next week, someone helped themselves to the engine and gearbox. Another night, all the mahogany vanished. What remained of the sunken boat was now a pile of drying wood in the public parking lot, just outside the Gordon Park fence.

A few weeks later, just after dark, the woodpile went up in flames. The Fire Department showed up, but they decided to just let it burn itself out. It made a beautiful bonfire.

Junior and I stood together watching the flames, which licked high into the air. At times, little fire tornados twirled in and out of the blaze. I looked at Junior and saw the hint of a smile.

"You did it, didn't you? You started the fire," I said.

"Why would you think that?"

"You did it," I repeated. "Otherwise you'd have asked me if I started the fire."

Junior didn't say another word while turning his gaze back to the fire. I did the same.

CHAPTER 17: MEMORIAL DAY

At our request, Junior let us move our berth from the east side of Pier One to the west side. That effectively put the pier between us and the public boat launching ramps. Last season, no fewer than five errant boats from the ramps banged into our hull. We wanted to avoid that situation in the future. Taking Hank's old slip, he moved his boat over to the next pier.

Junior rented our former slip to two new customers. One went to a sixteen-foot fiberglass fishing boat and the other to a twenty-six-foot *Revel Craft.* The cruiser, named the *Mary Margaret,* was owned by a steelworker named John.

John looked to be about twenty-five. He worked the overnight shift at *Republic Steel* and every morning after work, he showed up and slept on his boat until about three in the afternoon. A personable guy, John liked to drink beer and talk, in that order. Aside from fishing with his father once or twice a month, John's boat rarely left the marina.

Junior improved his docks by installing two lights on the posts at the end of the piers. The lights attracted thousands of small fish, I think they were eating the vegetation growing on the pier supports.

One night while sitting on our rear deck we heard a splash behind the boat and turned to see big ripples radiating from the pier post. Puzzled by the incident at first, we went back to passing the joint and *shooting-the-shit.* Then, a few minutes later Kris, John, and I were shocked to see a mouth half-a-foot wide, come out of the water! It was a huge carp that was feeding on the little pier-post-fish.

There were few more sightings of *King Carp,* as we came to call him. John wanted to catch that fish real bad. He showed up a few days later with a homemade harpoon. It was a first-class job. He'd made it out of a five-foot-long broomstick with a ten-inch steel-barbed spear attached to one end, and a retrieval rope on the other.

John threw his harpoon at *King Carp* a few times over the next few days, never hitting him even once. In an act of defiance, he sat at the end of the pier in a lawn chair waiting patiently for King Carp. With a beer cooler by his side, and his trusty harpoon at the ready, he vowed to catch the big fish.

We started calling John, "Captain Ahab"—how could you not?

While playing rummy in the cabin the next night, we heard John shout out "I got him! I got him!"

We ran to the rear deck in time to see about three feet of the broomstick, sticking vertically out of the water, shaking violently back and forth. Then the harpoon snapped, the handle broke away from the spearhead, and a dejected John reeled it in.

The next morning while having coffee on the rear deck, I heard a commotion in the launch ramp area. Standing, I saw *King Carp* floating on his side near the ramps. Some guy using a boat hook attached to a line snagged the big fish and was pulling him in. I went over and told him the story about the dead carp. He said it was *his* fish now.

"I don't care about the fish, but I'd like to get John's harpoon tip back to him."

He pulled the metal tip out of the fish and handed it to me. *King Carp* was much larger than I imagined, I didn't think there were fish that big in Lake Erie. The guy said the carp would feed his family for a week. I suggested eating a fish he found floating dead in a marina, might not be a wise idea. It didn't seem to matter to him. He took the big fish to the bait shop where it weighed in at a shade under fifty pounds and measured thirty-six inches long. Junior took a picture for John, saying, "I've seen a lot of big carp, but this may be the largest."

* * *

As the weather improved, the marina regulars returned to Gordon Park, including a few new boat owners.

One night, a new couple at the marina had a loud argument. It seemed the wife paid a surprise visit to their boat, only to discover her husband with another woman. We couldn't help but overhear their yelling, when all of a sudden, POP, POP, POP, POP! Shots rang out intermixed with screaming.

Everyone dove for cover! Then hearing Hank intercede, we ran to see if we could help as well. The wife was hit in the forehead by a beer bottle and was bleeding profusely. The three were sloppy drunk and engaged in a bloody brawl, fighting like cats and dogs. Blood was everywhere, so it took a few minutes to determine if anyone was hit by a bullet, luckily they weren't.

After we separated them, Hank unloaded the revolver and convinced the wife to let him hold on to the remaining two bullets.

We left after that, but the yelling continued for a quarter hour, ending when a car left the parking lot, spinning a shower of gravel from its tires. The next weekend, the two were back together but their loud, drunken arguments continued through the summer. Thankfully without the gunplay.

In early June, Kris answered the boat phone and took down a message for me. The call came from Mollie, the attractive paint clerk I'd met two months earlier at *Uncle Bill's*. I called her back and she told me that she'd broken up with her boyfriend and wanted to know if my offer for a boat ride still stood.

The following Saturday morning, Mollie and her

girlfriend, Mary Ann, joined Norm, Kris, his date, and me for a fun day on the lake. Mollie brought a picnic-style lunch for everyone and we headed east up the coast to a secluded little beach near the Chagrin River. We dropped anchor fifty-feet offshore and waded in.

Blue skies, white puffy clouds, a private beach, and pretty girls. These were the makings of a fun day. We piled up driftwood for an evening bonfire, then spent the day swimming, sunbathing, talking, and partying.

Later, a deep amber sunset gave way to twilight and a bright moonlit night. After our driftwood fire, we headed to *Captain Frank's* for a late night snack. It would be a two-hour boat ride, then another hour back to Gordon Park. That night, I really appreciated the boats slow speed. In fact, I even set the throttle a little slower than usual. Savoring each minute, I didn't want the night to end.

While Norm and Mary Ann didn't hit it off, Mollie and I continued dating.

CHAPTER 18: CANADA

Across the lake on the Canadian shore, Rondeau Bay and the small village of Erieau, lay roughly sixty miles to the north. One of the marina people who visited the area described it as untouched. He said the bay provided a glimpse of Lake Erie in its original state. Clearwater and natural forests had evolved without the influence of an industrialized society.

I wanted to see what that looked like, both above and below the water. My limited scuba diving experience had all been done around Cleveland. Here the water clarity and objects within, reminded me of a dirty fish bowl. I wanted to experience a pristine underwater environment.

Depending on lake conditions, the crossing could take eight hours and we were looking forward to a new adventure. When Ivan loaned us his scuba gear, he warned me that we'd be crossing fifteen miles of heavily used shipping lanes. We had to be careful mid-lake, since 1,000 foot long iron-ore boats regularly traversed the lake at an average speed of twenty-knots. Our speed of six-knots meant we'd have to keep a watchful eye for cross-traffic. The following night, we topped off our fuel tank, ready to go to Canada in the morning.

Perry would join us for the crossing. Kris, Norm, Me, Bob, and Perry made up our core group. With or without girlfriends, we were a tight bunch.

Perry could have been the pattern for TV's *Fonz* persona. Years before the mid-seventies' television show *Happy Days* brought awareness to the kind-hearted, biker-type; Perry lived the part. He rode a motorcycle and always wore a black leather jacket, blue jeans, and engineer boots. He was "*The Fonz*" before there was a "*Fonz.*"

* * *

Checking the charts, we'd follow a heading of 340° to Erieau in Rondeau Bay. Depending on current and wind, that heading should get us close enough. A low-power AM radio station, CFCO, near Earieu will help pinpoint the village from about twenty miles out. I'm going to try and use a cheap transistor AM radio as a crude radio directional finder.

Since its internal ferrite loop antenna is more sensitive when it's broadside to the station's signal. By rotating the radio around its base I can identify its position when the station comes in best. The front of the radio will be facing the CFCO antenna near Erieau. The station operates from dawn to dusk, so we should be able to easily find Rondeau Bay.

Nice weather prevailed as we left for Canada, but once we lost sight of land, the waves got larger, the sky clouded over, and a heavy rain began to fall. Wind from the northeast pushed us westward, so I corrected our course with my best guess. This wasn't our first time in bad weather, so we put on our life-jackets and ponchos, except for Perry, who was a bit of a risk taker.

Perry sat on a barstool while he steered the boat. His life jacket draped across the instrument panel, he said, "It's handy if I need it."

Kris told Perry, "When it's rough, we usually stand behind the wheel for better balance. The barstool is more for calmer stuff."

"Don't worry about me," said Perry, "I've got terrific balance."

And he did. I've seen him stand upright on the seat of a motorcycle as it went down the road. Or lying flat-out like Superman on Route 322 doing eighty. Just watching him do crazy shit like that, drew my nuts up into my belly sending chills through my gut.

In our third hour, a large freighter crossed our path less than a half-mile ahead, but we could barely make out its shape in the rain. The reduced visibility and our close call with the freighter persuaded us to immediately turn back to Cleveland.

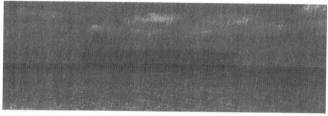

Lake Freighter barely visible in the rain

I told Perry to turn left to 160°, reversing our course, then I went into the cabin to get a sandwich. As I returned to the rear deck, the freighter's large and unexpected wake caught up with us. The barstool holding Perry rocked first toward the centerline, then snapped back like a pendulum using Perry's own momentum to launch him toward the lake. I dropped my sandwich and grabbed for his leg, but missed. However, our roof support, a two-inch-wide vertical iron pipe, deflected Perry onto the rear deck, saving his *too-cool for a life-jacket* ass.

Going overboard in bad weather is a dangerous situation. We'd have to make a complete turn to rescue him. That could take 3-minutes in good conditions, but with 2-to-3-foot waves, it could take a lot more time. We might not even be able to find him in the choppy water without a life jacket.

That experience left Perry with a badly bruised shoulder. I helped him into a life-jacket, then used duct tape to secure his arm in a makeshift sling taped directly to the life-vest. Immobilizing his arm helped with the pain.

As we continued southward, the weather improved. Although we were thankful for the sunshine and calmer conditions, we felt disappointed that we didn't make it to Canada. We'd probably try the Canadian trip again in a month or two.

I blamed myself for bad planning and not checking Canadian weather conditions before departure. Mistakes like that can prove fatal, and the close call with the freighter left a lasting impression.

Ivan suggested that in the future, during bad weather, we trail a hundred-foot knotted safety line behind us. That way, anyone who fell overboard would at least have a chance to grab the line.

Once back at Gordon Park, Norm drove Perry to the emergency room. His arm and the orange life vest bound tightly together by duct tape. He was not a happy camper, this wasn't a respectable look for a biker like Perry.

CHAPTER 19:
FIREWORKS DERECHO

A friend of Ivan's told me about a secluded *boat-in* resort on one of the Lake Erie islands, north of Cedar Point.

"Put-in-Bay, it's a party town, only accessible by water." he said, "It's kind of a secret spot where boaters go to let loose and have a good time. The place is legendary. It's on South Bass Island."

That sparked my interest, so I asked around. It turned out the place had a hedonistic reputation. Put-in-Bay was known as a come-for-the-fun harbor town that catered to the summer boating crowds. Sounds like our kind of people. It was unanimous, we'd visit Put-in-Bay on our upcoming Independence Day trip to Cedar Point.

Just before sunset on July first, I stood at the wheel as we came around the eastern side of South Bass Island. The bay was big and beautiful, hundreds of pleasure-craft lined the shores. This was unlike anything I'd ever seen. I slowed to marina speed and wove our way through the crowded harbor. Half hidden through the forest of masts was the town of Put-in-Bay itself, occupying a quarter-mile strip in the center of the mile-wide bay.

All of the available dock space in town was occupied at five-times capacity. Boats were tied side-by-side extending into the bay like fingers on a glove. Each of the boats was secured to the next separated by dock-bumpers. We found a place to connect-up at the end of a five-boat stack. Of course, getting to shore and back required climbing across neighboring boats. It sounds intrusive, but surprisingly, the action added fun and camaraderie to the island experience. At 35-feet, the *Day Tripper* was the largest craft in our group.

The stacking of boats, or "rafting", as the regulars call it, is a usual weekend occurrence in Put-in-Bay. The town didn't have lodging to support the influx of tourists on busy weekends. There were a couple of small hotels, a popular local winery, restaurants, a well-stocked grocery market, and five or six bars.

This little harbor-town quickly brought on a festive mood. A nice mix of laid-back older and younger boaters who came to the bay with one thought: *Let's party!* People let their hair down and had fun. There's an old expression on the island; "What happens in Put-in-Bay, stays in Put-in-Bay."

At the winery, our first stop, we hooked up with a Detroit group of six that came down on a large sailboat. Good times ensued, lots of wine, smoke, and boisterous conversations. Next thing I knew, It was dawn and we were leaving their sailboat after a night of partying.

July second was all about sightseeing. Put-in-Bay had an interesting history relating to The War of 1812. A distinctive landmark on the island is the 350' tall Commodore Oliver Hazard Perry Victory Monument. The structure's observation deck offered a view of the horizon that included Canada to the north and Sandusky to the south. A spectacular sight, especially on this cloudless day. The park ranger, stationed on the deck told us about the monument's significance and the nearby battle it represented.

That afternoon we walked into the large Round House Bar, where we joined up with some people from Grosse Pointe, Michigan. A terrific local band played, the food was good and drinks kept coming. I ended up in a backgammon game with a super-hot older lady. We all went to the winery and ended up finishing up the evening on their cabin cruiser.

After a shit-load of partying and two nights without meaningful sleep, we left Put-in-Bay on our way to the next port of call, Cedar Point. Mollie and a couple of her girlfriends were driving up to join me and the guys. We'd all watch the fireworks on the forth, from the deck of the *Day Tripper*. Mollie planned to stay with me on the boat for two nights, including the ride back to Cleveland.

Before going to Cedar Point, we'd make a short detour inspired by our visit to the 1812 Victory Monument. Three miles northwest of Put-in-Bay, we came around the far side of Rattlesnake Island.

Once there, we cut the engine and drifted quietly. This is the spot. The surface of the lake was flat as bathwater and the only sounds came from distant outboard motors. But on September 10, 1813, this was a fierce battlefield.

In a bloody five-hour engagement, US Naval Commander Oliver Hazard Perry, on the brig Niagara defeated the British fleet on this very spot. He captured six vessels of the Royal Navy and ensured American control of the Great Lakes and the recovery of Detroit. It would be known as The Battle of Lake Erie. Commander Perry dispatched one of the most famous messages in naval history. It read: *"We have met the Enemy, and they are ours."*

Continuing around Rattlesnake Island, we approached Cedar Point from the north this time, around Marblehead peninsula. Berthing in our favorite slip at the marina, we spent most of the first day catching up on sleep. Tomorrow Mollie and her friends would be here.

On the fourth, we awoke to a beautiful day—sunny and humid with a predicted high of eighty-two degrees, perfect summer weather and a great beginning to the Independence Day weekend.

As the day progressed, people did their usual holiday things: partying on boats, backyards, beaches, and parks. They grilled hot dogs, ribs, chickens, and burgers. Later, families would head to the coast to watch the evening's entertainment—the big firework displays along the lakeshore.

However, late in the afternoon, unknown to anyone in Northern Ohio, storm clouds were building fast over southeast Michigan, forming into giant stacks 60,000 feet high. Then they began moving east. Once over the lake, the brewing storm turned and sped toward Sandusky and Cedar Point where the giant amusement park hosted a capacity crowd for the holiday weekend.

If the weather watchers in Detroit knew a severe storm was forming, they didn't alert anyone in Ohio—a mistake that would cause many fatalities.

At 7:15 PM, the National Weather Service told the Emergency Broadcast System to standby; weather conditions would soon be upgraded to a full-force gale or tornado. Then mistakenly, the warning was never issued!

7:30: On the sidewalk next to the boat, I set up our small Weber grill and lit the charcoal briquettes. Kris and Norm walked to the marina store for hot dog buns.

7:35: The captain of a freighter ten miles north of Put-In-Bay was the first to report 110 mile-per-hour winds and heavy rain heading toward shore. His alert would be the *only* forewarning.

7:45: The storm made landfall at Marblehead and Cedar Point as many pleasure boats headed into Sandusky Bay, getting ready to watch the evening's big fireworks display.

I had just placed six hot dogs on the grill when I noticed the sky had darkened. As the first strong breeze rushed through the marina, I turned to see Kris and Norm running towards me at full speed. Winds increased as leaves, branches, garbage cans, and other debris began to blow past me. Our grill fell over and blew away.

The ferocity of a wind gust almost knocked me over as I stumbled for my footing. Then I heard what sounded like the roar of a freight train as an explosive blistering downpour, turned horizontal hit hard and fast. The rain stung like small stones thrown hard against bare skin.

What the hell is happening?

Rain combined with category-three hurricane-force winds was like nothing I had ever experienced, expected, or imagined. We climbed aboard and hoped for the best.

7:50 PM: The force of the storm continuously slammed the *Day Tripper* hard into the seawall breaking a ten-foot section of the thick wood edging along our port gunwale. We tried to go out and reposition our bumpers, but the storm's intensity drove us back into the cabin. We'd fix the damage later, there was no going out into that weather.

Tying along the seawall, which was higher than our deck, caused the gunwale to take the brunt of the pounding. From our perspective, it was frightening. Even with a steel hull, we questioned whether the boat could take the rough treatment, and for how long? If rivets started popping, we could quickly sink.

My concerns included Mollie. Two of her friends were driving her to meet me at the marina, they were due about the time all hell broke loose with the weather.

As the storm rushed through northern Ohio, one after another, trees fell upending their roots. The worst of the storm lasted an hour, but combined with twelve additional hours of gale-force winds, rain, and flooding, it was recorded as the deadliest storm to have ever hit the area. It would be known as "The Ohio Fireworks Derecho"

When the storm eased up, we went outside to inspect the damage. Three dock-bumpers were destroyed, but only about twelve-feet of our gunwale facing board was damaged, *better than I thought.*

With the storm still going strong, we made a decision to reposition the boat, moving it from its windward location against the seawall to an open slip twenty feet away where the wind would hold us off the pier structure, instead of pushing us into it.

Three of our neighbors, who were also out adjusting their lines, volunteered to help us move the boat, and lucky for us they did. We couldn't have done it without them.

The move was only twenty-feet laterally. There were six of us with lines attached to the boat from two sides. Our three helpers were positioned on the sidewalk/seawall side, Norm, Kris, and I stood on the dock and pulled the boat toward us. Working those lines felt like we were trying to control a huge angry bull that wouldn't cooperate. In the end, it took all of us pulling from the docks to finally secure the boat. Way more difficult than I ever imagined.

Sleep wasn't easy. The *Day Tripper* pitched and tugged at its lines. Twice I rolled off the couch onto the floor, finally electing to stay put. At least down here, I'd be the first to know if we took on water.

The next morning, I awoke on the floor. The storm had stopped and I was glad to see we were still afloat. Everything felt damp including me. The cabin was humid and muggy; there was no air circulation. I got up, opened the windows, and went outside to survey the damage. On this a gray dismal morning, a light drizzle fell while chainsaws buzzed as work crews cleared fallen trees.

I took a look at the port gunwale and the wood rub-rail where it contacted the seawall. We'd have to replace three five-foot sections along the thirty-five-foot rail. All-in-all, I was impressed. Inside, we removed floor and wall panels to check if any rivets were missing, everything looked okay.

Not far from the boat a tree had fallen across the chain link fence that separated the amusement park from the marina. A maintenance crew was busy untangling power lines from downed branches.

On my way to the pay-phones, I began to see the aftermath of the massive storm. Tree limbs lay everywhere. Garbage, chairs, and trash lay flat against chain-link fences. Cleanup crews were hard at work doing a job that looked overwhelming.

The line for the phone booths must have been sixty feet long. While in line, someone had a radio, and it revealed the severity of last night's *mother of all thunderstorms*. It was far worse than anyone imagined. I was shocked. Over forty people were dead in three states, 250,000 in the region were without power, hundreds of vacationers on the Lake Erie Islands were missing or stranded, 5,000 trees fell, and more than 100 boats were missing.

Someone said fifteen boats in the marina sank overnight, right in their slips. After the punishment the *Day Tripper* took from banging against the seawall, I was glad we weren't among them. It took almost two hours before I got to a phone.

My parents had been beside themselves with worry. By the time I got through to them, it was 10 AM. My mother had been up all night. The morning TV News report talked about all the missing boats at Cedar Point. When they didn't get a call from me first thing in the morning, she feared the worst. My father said he'd contact Kris and Norm's parents, who they'd been in touch with throughout the night.

Next, I called Mollie, who had arrived home just minutes before her phone rang. She told me they got to the Cedar Point Causeway just after the storm hit. The causeway closed down and everyone had to turn around and go back. Fallen trees blocked the only road to the amusement park and marina. The ride back to Cleveland took them all night due to flooding, detours, and downed trees.

* * *

That night we were invited for dinner aboard a neighboring boat, a forty-four-foot trawler with two couples from Toledo. We told our boating stories, they told theirs. They were interesting people and we got along well.

They were heading back to Toledo in the morning. The skipper said "Waves and rain don't stop me, it shouldn't stop you either. Your fricken hull is a double-ended lifeboat made for rough ocean conditions, and this ain't no ocean."

After a few bottles of wine, we convinced ourselves that he was right; we'd head home in the morning as well. After all, we had a fricken double-ender. Lake Erie at its worst should be a piece of cake. Being young, stupid, and full of wine-induced bravado, we planned to leave for Cleveland in the morning.

It's unclear why the red small-craft advisory flag wasn't on the marina's flagpole. We looked for it as we motored past. If the flag had been displayed, we likely would not have gone.

"Look," I pointed out, "there's no red flag, were good to go."

We didn't know it then, but the missing flag was an oversight; a small-craft warning had been issued.

Kris was at the controls as we ran parallel to the Sandusky breakwall, heading out toward open water. The waves didn't look so big at first, but by the time we realized how big they actually were, we were already in the thick of it. We motored head-on into the largest waves I had ever seen! I knew right then we were in deep trouble. Turning back, our only good option would be difficult. We'd have to negotiate a 180^0 turn within the trough between two wave crests. If we got caught broadside in the turn, we would likely capsize.

Norm and I went to the bow, looking for a break between the waves so we could complete our turn back to Cedar Point. The bow rose skyward as we crested each oncoming wave and dropped hard into the troughs between them. As the pounding continued our refrigerator broke away from its bulkhead mount and began tumbling freely inside the cabin. It damaged everything it slammed into. Hearing the crashing and imagining the damage, I re-cinched my life-jacket straps. *I hope I don't need this.*

Then our gap in the waves appeared! I motioned to Kris, circling my hand above my head like I held a lasso. He spun the wheel and applied full power. Once we committed to the turn, there was no going back. We hadn't yet come completely around when the next wave arrived sooner than we would have liked.

The *Day Tripper* rolled hard on its port side, the gunwale dipped low into the water. I thought we were going over. As the wave moved under our keel, the hull quickly righted itself.

Norm and I clung tightly to the bow rail as the momentum of the rolling hull tried to fling us into the lake. I was also glad to see that Kris hung-on at the wheel.

The *Day Tripper* was thirty-five feet long and twelve-feet wide, it displaced over eighteen tons, but those waves tossed us around like a toy. Then another problem arose. In the heavy following sea, waves overtaking us lifted our stern, exposing the prop and over-revving the engine. Kris had to constantly adjust the throttle to keep the engine from speeding-up when the prop was briefly out of the water.

As we approached the safety of the breakwall and Sandusky Bay, wave height diminished. Then, as I watched in disbelief, a wooden speed-boat came toward us, heading out into the lake, *were they crazy?*

As the speedboat jumped over the wave tops, the three aboard seemed to enjoy the excitement of the ride. They waved as we passed each other. I motioned and yelled for them to turn around but they paid no heed. Soon they would find themselves in some serious shit. One of them held up a beer can and none wore life jackets.

I suspected we'd be the last people to see them alive.

Back in bay waters, I entered the cabin. It was a mess. The tumbling refrigerator did a lot of damage, spilling its contents, breaking apart, and tearing upholstery.

With the boat secured back in our slip, we went to the marina restaurant for lunch. All the food we had onboard was ruined, scattered across the floor like someone had emptied a trash bag. A piece of bologna was stuck right in the middle of the forward cabin window.

Returning from lunch, we were shocked to find the boat sitting low and three inches of water covering the cabin floor. Neither of our two automatic bilge pumps was running! Our spare battery, which powered both pumps, had torn loose from its bracket in the big waves, disconnecting its wires.

Something had to be done fast, the *Day Tripper* was sinking!

A nearby boater seeing our predicament offered us the use of his portable pump and we ran to get it on the next pier. By the time the pump was set up and running, the water had risen to six-inches in the cabin. The high-capacity pump drained the hull in a couple of hours.

Once the water was sucked out, it wasn't difficult to pinpoint the leak. I could hear the sound of splashing under the floorboards in the front cabin. Pulling back the waterlogged carpet, I lifted the floor planks and there, spouting from the hull, was a finger-thick column of water that looked a little like the flow from a drinking fountain.

Kris grabbed a rag and held it over the leak with his foot. I ran to the store to see if they had something that would fix it. We were in luck; they actually had a hull patch kit.

Putting on a diving mask, I swam under the bow to prep the area around the leak. The small hole wasn't hard to find and I roughed-up the area where I'd be applying the underwater epoxy.

With the hull ready, Norm handed me a paint scraper with a quarter-sized glob of pre-mixed epoxy stuck to it. Kris held the leak at bay with the rag under his foot while I spread an even layer of epoxy from underwater. It took 60 minutes to set. When Kris removed his foot, the leak had all but stopped. We sanded the inside of the hull around the breach and added two more layers of epoxy, both inside the hull and outside. It would take two days for the epoxy patch to develop its full strength.

Evidence at the site of the leak pointed to its cause. Normal hull vibrations and a rusted old wrench found next to the hole appeared to have been the culprit. The head of the wrench had abraded-away a dime-sized section of the hull's protective zinc galvanized coating. Without the coating, the raw steel rusted. The weakened area must have broken through from the stress and pounding of the crashing waves earlier in the day.

By the afternoon we'd removed everything wet from the cabin. Clothes, blankets, and towels were cleaned and dried at the marina Laundromat Everything else got laid on top of the cabin to dry. Fortunately, the long-range forecast called for sunshine.

CHAPTER 20: THREE COP CARS

The epoxy had to cure, but we had jobs to get to. Norm stayed on the boat while Kris and I hitchhiked to Gordon Park to get my car. We'd pick up Perry and head back to Cedar Point for Norm.

Perry agreed to stay onboard alone and watch the boat until the following weekend. We'd return after the epoxy had cured and bring the *Day Tripper* home.

At dark, Kris and I walked the length of the five-mile causeway bridge connecting the amusement park to the main highway. We'd thumb our way east along coastal Route 6 all the way to Cleveland, a distance of sixty miles.

Our first ride came quickly, but with storm-related road closures, we ended up in an undeveloped district south of Lorain. This was not where we planned to be.

The driver dropped us off on Broadway Avenue. He said it ran north for seven miles ending at Route 6.

Walking for a while along almost deserted streets, we reached a residential area. Late night traffic was scarce and it didn't look like a safe neighborhood. Finally, a car approached. I stuck out my thumb and it veered to the curb stopping beside us. It was a shiny black convertable, a '62 Chevy low-rider.

Inside there were four occupants, one opened the passenger door and we got in. I sat in the back and Kris took the front shotgun seat.

"Thanks for the ride," I said, "are you going to Route 6?"

No response, everyone stayed quiet. I was a little concerned.

He either ignored my question or didn't understand English. We proceeded *slowly* north on Broadway. I got bad vibes from these guys, and why the hell were they driving so damn slow? Now, I had misgivings about getting in the car. Were we going to be robbed?

Everyone remained eerily silent as we drove north. Then, the guy next to me yelled to the driver, "Chacho, pull over, there's fuckin' Jimmy!"

He pointed to a man standing in a lit doorway to the right. The driver quickly turned toward the curb, stopped and tapped his horn. Jimmy came over and leaned slightly into the rear window. He spoke to the guy on my left, saying something about next week. Suddenly the guy grabs Jimmy by the shirt and pulls him inward, right across me! He yelled something angrily in Spanish, then pushes Jimmy out of the car. Jimmy takes out his wallet and extends it toward me. I pass it to the left. With the cash removed, the wallet is tossed out the window and we drove away.

The guys spoke to each other in Spanish, they seemed agitated. Then Kris pulled out a joint, lit it, and took a long hit. The talking stopped and their eyes lock on Kris. Seconds later he exhaled, passed the joint to his left, and said, "Fuckin' Jimmy."

Everyone busts-up laughing. The comment and joint eased the tension. Kris always knew the right thing to say—he could schmooze anyone.

When the laughter dwindled, the driver, previously silent, said he'd take us to the Route 6. After that, I relaxed a bit, no longer feeling we'd be robbed.

Getting out of the low-rider, Kris handed the roach to the guys and the black lowrider turned south, disappearing slowly into the coastal fog.

We walked east along the coast road for about a mile before we caught a ride. I remember a lot of walking that evening, traffic was scarce and the road was storm damaged. Downed branches and uprooted trees were on every block. Trunks that blocked the roadway had simply been cut away, cleanup would come later. A few more rides and by daybreak we walked into the affluent town of Bay Village, a bedroom community west of Cleveland. Up ahead, a local police car coming toward us made a quick U-turn and stopped in in our path.

Shit, are we were going to be arrested for hitchhiking? To my amazement, the officer said he'd drive us through Bay Village to the next city. We cautiously got into the back seat of his police car. Although in my mind, I was still thinking we were going to be arrested and the offer to drive us to the next city was a ruse.

Along the way, I explained what happened at Cedar Point. Ten minutes later he dropped us off at the next little town, Rocky River. "Unless they were busy," he said, "One of their patrol cars would pick us up and drive us to Lakewood, the last coastal city before Cleveland. We thanked him for the ride and for setting up the police-car relay.

Once on the sidewalk, we stared at each other in disbelief. Did that really happen?

Minutes later, a Rocky River police cruiser pulled up and we climbed into the back seat. *Unbelievable.*

At the next city, Lakewood, another police car was already waiting for us. These guys were great. I wondered if all hitchhikers got this special treatment.

The Lakewood cop took us to the on-ramp of the Cleveland Municipal Shoreway. That was the freeway that runs right past Gordon Park Marina, where I'd left my car a week earlier. Our last ride dropped us at the 72nd Street off-ramp and we walked the last quarter-mile to the marina. As we drove off to pick up Perry, Kris said, "No one is gonna believe the crazy-shit from last night."

* * *

After a stopping at our banks, we picked up Perry and headed back to Cedar Point. By the time we got to the boat, we were ready to collapse from lack of sleep.

Perry brought some comforts from home, his 16-inch portable black and white TV, a radio, and a couple of books.

I left him with thirty dollars for food, and Kris, Norm, and I departed for Cleveland. Norm drove, Kris and I slept.

The following Friday evening, Bob drove Kris and me back to Cedar Point. Perry was watching a new TV show called Playboy after Dark, broadcast from a television station in Detroit. With Hefner, celebrities, and Playboy Bunnies, how could this show not be great?

In the morning Bob and Perry drove back to Cleveland. Kris and I breakfasted at the restaurant and bought some food, beverages, and snacks for the boat ride home. Fighting a slight headwind, it took us thirteen hours to get to Gordon Park.

This last trip had been memorable, running the gamut from good times partying at Put-in-Bay, to hurricane force winds. Including the terror of nearly capsizing in storm-whipped waves.

We got right to work repairing the *Day Tripper*. Storm damage inside the cabin included broken cabinets and torn upholstery. All done by the tumbling refrigerator. On the exterior, fifteen feet of gunwale rub-rail needed replacing.

There's an old nautical saying; "A boat is safe in a harbor—but that's not what boats are for."

CHAPTER 21: THE RICHARDSON

Mollie and I began dating exclusively. We were together nearly every weekend. She enjoyed hanging out at the boat and helped us with the repairs as well. Her upholstery experience came in handy when she made new blue vinyl cushions for the couch and dinette seats.

Norm found us a nice replacement refrigerator at a boat salvage yard. Although a bit larger than the original, Ivan would make sure the replacement fridge fit into the new cabinet unit that he built from scratch.

Ivan set up a table saw at the foot of our pier. With it, and a few simple tools, he built us new cabinets and drawers. Ivan's many skills never failed to impress. He could do anything.

With new cabinets, upholstery, and fresh paint, the *Day Tripper* was in better shape than ever.

* * *

On a hot August night, Kris, Norm, Bob, and I all took dates to Fagans, a popular waterfront restaurant in the Flats. As we tied our dock-lines, a man approached and asked me if we bought our boat from a yard on the Chagrin River?

I turned to see a gray-haired 50-ish guy, wearing white shorts, a blue T-shirt, and sporting a black baseball cap. His tanned skin, cap, and topsiders shouted yachtsman.

"Yeah, John's Boatyard, we bought it the beginning of last year," I said.

He extended his hand.

"I'm Carl. I saw this boat about eight years ago when it first showed up at the boatyard, and I'm especially happy to see it here today."

He explained, "I was at John's Boatyard the day the lifeboat arrived. An older foreign fellow bought it from a surplus sale in Buffalo. I talked to him for a while, nice guy, a carpenter I think. The boat was big, empty, and gray. It was nothing but a hull with an engine, all the lifeboat stuff was stripped out, just the hull and the motor, nothing else.

"When I saw the boat the following year, the carpenter had finished the bulk of the build-out and everything had been painted in white primer. The year after that, the completed boat conversion looked basically the same as it does today. But through the next few years, the boat just sat there."

Carl was a member of the Chagrin Lagoons Yacht Club, located a quarter-mile down-river, just north of John's Boatyard.

He continued, "Years went by, windows were broken, trees and bushes grew around the boat. Last summer, when it was gone, I thought for sure it was scrapped."

He invited us to join his group of friends for dinner at Fagans, and we accepted. I told them how we ended up with the *Day Tripper* for fifty-dollars, but it was his stories I wanted to hear. Last summer, Carl and his wife sailed all the way around Lake Erie. That was a journey I had wanted to do, but none of us could afford the time off-work.

After dinner, we moved the party to the deck of his Tartan 37. Tartan Yachts are built locally in Fairport Harbor, east of Cleveland. They are world-class yachts.

Later that evening, he told us about a boat for sale at his yacht club. "It's a 38-foot Richardson Salon Cruiser. Built in 1945. The hull is double-planked mahogany, it has a central salon, and both forward and aft cabins."

He went on, "A deceased member's family donated the boat to the yacht club. The Richardson sat in a cradle, out of the water for the past four years.

"The club wants it gone. I know they'd take three-grand, maybe less."

* * *

It was just before dawn as the *Day Tripper*, damp with morning dew, carried us home after a long night partying on the river. By the time we passed *Captain Frank's*, the sun cleared the horizon bathing the city in a beautiful orange hue.

Photographers call this the *golden hour*, everything looks better bathed in this softer, amber, morning light. Daybreak on the waterfront holds a special serenity for me. The sounds of screeching gulls above and the engine's constant speed, droning below my feet, felt like music to my ears.

I was the only one awake and we still had an hour ride to Gordon Park. I hoped that someone else will be up by the time we get there to help with the lines. Ten minutes later, I was happy to see cabin door open and Mollie came out.

"You want some company?"

"I sure do."

Snuggling against my side, she wrapped a blanket around us to stave off the morning chill. It looked to be the beginning of a beautiful day.

* * *

The next afternoon, Kris, Norm, and I drove to the Chagrin Lagoons Yacht Club to have a look at the Richardson. It was a big boat, a custom-built luxury yacht that looked to be in good condition. Carl said it was one of two identical boats, built as sister-ships.

He propped a ladder against the side of the boat and we climbed aboard. Entering the main salon through a sliding side-door, my first view was impressive. To my left, a built-in red leather couch almost filled the salon's back wall. Beyond that, a curved stairway took you down to the aft cabin. It had a double bed, small couch, a dresser, and full bathroom. A door on the far wall opened to the small-ish rear deck.

Back in the salon, on the port side, a leather captain's chair sat in front of a well-appointed instrument panel. On the starboard side, a chart table topped a cabinet housing navigation charts and instruments. Two Chrysler straight-eight motors below the salon's deck, powered the big boat.

Moving forward from the salon and down a few steps, a short hall led to the forward cabin. The hall divided the room, the galley to starboard, and a full bathroom to port. The forward cabin slept four.

The boat had an old smell, but that was understandable since it had sat for so long. Thankfully, there was no odor of mildew, so the deck was sound and kept the inside dry.

We spent a couple of hours checking the boat from stem to stern. I told Carl we would be back tomorrow with a battery and some tools. If the engines start, we'd probably make an offer.

The next morning Bob met us at Gordon Park, and we drove to Chagrin Lagoons, an hour away. We brought along two batteries, an assortment of tools, jumper cables, and a compression gauge. It was our understanding that both engines ran four years ago. We hoped they would start today.

Carl met us at the boat and let us aboard. Bob and I got right to work on the engines, Kris and Norm began checking the hull for dry rot. First we removed, cleaned, and gapped the spark plugs. Bob squirted a big shot of kerosene into each cylinder. Then pre-cranking the starter motor, he made sure that lubrication got into all the essential places. Bob also checked the compression of the cylinders. Seven were within an acceptable range, but one registered low. Bob suggested a sticking valve might be the problem; after all the engine sat for a long time. He'd recheck the compression later after the engine warmed up. Hopefully, he'd get a better reading.

With points set and the spark plugs back in, it was time to give it a go. Kris, standing between the engines, poured a little gas into the throat of the port carburetors, he looked up at me in the captain's chair, and said, "Give her a go."

I set the throttle a little above idle, pulled the choke to half and pushed the starter button. The port engine cranked for a full five seconds before sputtering, then it started and ran a few seconds before it quit.

Bob played around with the carburetors for an hour, then said, "Let's try to start it again; this time give it full-choke."

I pressed my thumb down hard on the chrome starter button, and within seconds, the engine came to life. It ran a little rough at first but smoothed out after a minute. It was firing on all eight cylinders.

To keep the engine from overheating, I could only let it run until the head got hot, maybe ten minutes. The engines normally draw their cooling water from an intake port on the bottom of the hull and that couldn't happen on land.

After preparing the starboard engine the same way, it started and ran smooth nearly right from the get-go. Over that afternoon, we restarted both engines a few more times. Both of the gearboxes operated as expected and re-testing compression of the port engine yielded good results.

Confident that the running gear was operational and the hull did not exhibit any signs of dry rot, we told Carl we were ready to make an offer.

An hour later he returned with the yacht club Commodore; we offered him $2,000 for the Richardson. He said he felt $3,000 was a fair price and they wouldn't take less. Carl pulled him aside; they talked a few minutes, and came back with a counteroffer of meeting in the middle at $2,500. We agreed. $300 and a handshake sealed the deal.

"We'll be ready to go in the water within a week or two." Kris told him.

Now we had to sell the *Day Tripper*. We did have a good lead though; an old friend of Hank's named Larry, expressed interest in buying the boat only a few weeks ago. He told us if we ever thought of selling, to give him first crack at it.

Hank called Larry, who came right over. He was interested and excited as well. That evening Larry steered the boat past downtown and back while we discussed the sale. Back at the marina, we agreed on a price. While asking $3,500, we settled for twenty-eight.

Larry handed us two hundred dollars; he'd bring the balance tomorrow. It was a bittersweet moment. We'd had a lot of good times aboard that boat, and even when we were dumb enough to go out in severe weather, the *Day Tripper* always brought us home.

Talk about things happening fast, four days earlier we had no plans of selling the boat; now it was a done deal. Overall, except for the expenses to prepare the Richardson, we were up $300 on the sale and owned a

38-foot twin-screw yacht free and clear. All that, parlayed from an original $50 purchase.

The *Day Tripper* had become such an integral part of our daily lives, I wondered if we'd miss it. But, at that moment, all I could think about was the new boat.

Larry paid me the balance, I signed over the title and handed him the keys. Junior assigned him a slip at the end of pier five. Larry and I moved the *Day Tripper* to the new slip. I told him he would need some one-on-one instruction on handling the boat so we agreed to spend the next day together.

"Bring a helper," I said, "the *Day Tripper* is too big to handle alone. I'll meet you here at nine."

The next morning I arrived early at eight. Per our agreement, I painted over the name *Day Tripper* on both sides of the bow. It turned out to be more of an emotional experience than I thought it would be.

As the second coat dried, I sat on the rear deck and reminisced: *I thought about the time we were on our way back from Cedar Point. The lake was calm, and the sky was clear. Kris lay face down on a chaise lounge on the bow deck. Norm and I decided to sit on the hard top above the console, the highest place on the boat. From up here, we had an unobstructed of the entire horizon and it was beautiful. The problem was, we couldn't normally steer from that position. Our solution involved wrapping ropes in opposite directions around the steering wheel. I sat on the starboard side holding one rope; Norm sat to port with the other. We were able to easily make small steering corrections from up on top.*

Many years later, when Norm and I were reminiscing about the *Day Tripper* days, we both recalled that particular incident, when we sat on the hard top and steered with ropes.

Larry and his wife interrupted my day-dreaming when they arrived for their boating lesson. She untied the dock lines and climbed aboard. As Larry backed his new boat out of his slip, it pulled hard to port, a trait he would always need to expect. Per my instructions: when the bow cleared the pier, he shifted to forward, applied full left rudder and goosed the throttle a little to stop the boat's rotation. Then he proceeded forward, out of the marina and into the larger outer basin where we turned around and docked the boat back in Larry's slip on pier five. A fifteen-minute round trip.

That day we must have made over ten trips from his slip to the outer basin and back. There is no substitute for hands-on experience, so it was *dock and repeat* all day. They needed to learn how to handle the boat, and most importantly, to do it without running into anything. Larry was quick to learn the boat's operation and characteristics.

They also needed to understand how to handle docking lines, including knowledge of the three knots every boater should know: the cleat hitch, clove hitch, and bowline.

"Learn them well—they're the only ones you'll ever need," I said.

***

The following weekend, everyone we could muster, showed up at the yacht club to help paint and prep the Richardson. I refer to the boat as the Richardson, although that wasn't its name. Richardson was the manufacturer. I think the name on the transom was *Lilly Lou* or something like that. I removed it at my first opportunity. We would give the new boat a proper name, as soon as we could agree on one.

Bob and I changed the oil, cleaned the flame suppressors, replaced the filters, hoses, and adjusted the tension on the steering cables. After that, we siphoned-off the stale gasoline that remained in the 200-gallon tank. We would take on fresh fuel when the boat was in the water.

Each evening before the launch we were at the yacht club preparing the boat. There was no shortage of things to do and a lot of brass and mahohany that needed polishing.

Mollie cooked the first meal aboard the Richardson while it was still on dry land. She roasted a chicken with potatoes right in our own oven.

"The boat has a fricken oven! How cool is that?"

The evening of the launch, Bob and Perry picked us up and we drove together to Chagrin Lagoons to pick up the *new* boat. Perry said he wanted to be aboard for the maiden voyage and that was okay with us.

Once we got to the yacht club, the guys headed over to the back storage lot where the Richardson was located. I went looking around the grounds trying to locate Carl. I finally found him sitting in the clubhouse bar, about to down an inviting frosted mug of ice-cold draft beer.

"I'll have one too," I told the bartender. "It's too hot and humid to pass that up."

After downing our beers, Carl asked, "Ready to go get your boat?"

"I sure am."

"Let's get the *Travel-Lift*," he said.

We climbed a ladder to the mobile crane operating platform. Carl started the diesel engine, and off we went. This boat crane was twice the size of the one that launched the *Day Tripper*.

It felt odd driving a vehicle the size of a small

house. As we drove through a wooded area at dusk, hundreds of fireflies awakened filling the woods with little flashing yellow lights. I hadn't seen fireflies for many years –they were a welcome and enjoyable sight.

With a skilled hand, Carl steered the big crane into its lifting position straddling the boat. We climbed down, and he moved the two canvas-padded slings to the places where they would best support the hull. Then, back at the controls, he began to tighten the slings.

The cables and straps creaked and groaned as the full weight of the boat came to bear on the crane. Carl raised the hull two feet above its shoring-cradle and held it there as he locked the safety pins in each of the four winches. With the boat now securely attached to the crane, we began the slow trip from the storage yard to the launching pier. We followed the big rig, in Bob's car, as the boat, made its way slowly towards the water.

At the pier, Carl steered the crane's large tires into two parallel guide-channels atop twin concrete abutments. With the boat now hanging over the launch basin, he unlocked the safety pins, pulled a lever, and the Richardson descended slowly into the water. When the slings went slack, I inspected the bilge, water was seeping in but that was expected. As the dry hull planks absorb water and swell, the seepage should stop. By morning everything was okay.

I disconnected the strap latches on the two slings and they fell free of the hull. Giving Carl a thumbs-up signal, he started the winches retracting the slings while backing the crane off the pier.

Then he walked over and handed me a manila envelope, saying, "I almost forgot to give this to you."

Looking inside, I saw the boat's title and a few other documents. "Thanks; I'll put these in a safe place."

As he drove off on the *Travel-Lift*, I thought about how it was slightly over a week ago that we first met Carl. So much had gone down in that short amount of time.

Using ropes, the five of us moved the boat to the fuel dock on the next pier. An intercom near the pump brought an attendant in about ten minutes.

We took on 100 gallons of marine-grade gasoline, and the bill came to just under fifty-dollars. That was the most we ever paid for fuel.

Both engines started easily although one ran a little rough. Bob took apart the carburetors, made some adjustments, and in a couple of hours, both engines ran smooth.

Bob planned to leave after he finished with the engines. Instead, being a Friday night and almost eleven, he went to his car and returned with his trusty bamboo bong. Plans had changed.

At first light, someone knocked on the hull, I could hear a woman's voice call out, "Could you please move your boat out of the fuel dock?"

"Sorry, I'll get right to it," I replied.

I shook Bob, who had fallen asleep in the captain's chair. "Wake up! We need to move the boat."

I started the engines, Bob untied the docking lines and we motored over to the guest area and tied up. The twin screws made the boat easy to handle, even at low speed, when the rudders are usually less effective.

Kris and Norm had both awakened at this point, so we walked over to the clubhouse bar and ordered four breakfast specials, and one to go for the sleeping Perry.

Back on the boat, we did a another inspection of the bilge and things looked good. Bob rechecked the compression and all cylinders were operating within range. The boat is ready to go. When Bob left for home, he untied the dock lines, waved and shouted, "I'll see you later at Gordon Park."

I eased the Richardson slowly forward and out of the lagoon. Once in the river, I opened the throttles and the boat responded quickly. A few minutes later we were out in the lake turning west toward Cleveland. Running at twelve knots, I was mindful of Bob's suggestion to run the engines slower at first.

Operating the new boat from inside the salon turned out to be a very different experience from the

Day Tripper. It would take me a little time to get used to it.

A small breeze churned the lake into foot-tall choppy waves. The Richardson's full displacement hull, twin screws, and substantial weight allowed it to track smooth and steady, even through the chop.

Perry, finally awake, came into the salon to announce that he was the first one to use the bathroom on the new boat.

"Laughing, Kris said. "Number one, or number two? I gotta know for the logbook entry."

Perry chuckled, "I got your log—go see for yourself. With all the pedals and levers, I couldn't figure out how to flush the damn thing."

In his defense, the marine head, the toilet, was not an intuitive design. It required a few specialized procedures. You had to turn a valve, pump a foot-pedal, turn another valve, lift a knob, and pump the pedal again to clear the bowl. A brass-engraved wall plate detailed the operation. Perry must not have seen it.

CHAPTER 22:
THE BEGINNING OF THE END

The engines didn't miss a beat. Our first time on the lake with the new boat couldn't have went better. In a little under ninety-minutes, we passed-up the entrance to Gordon Park. Making good time, we decided to head to *Captain Frank's* for lunch.

Then, out of nowhere, Perry said lunch was on him. It got dead silent in the salon; we stared at each other in total disbelief. I don't think anyone had ever heard those words come out of Perry's mouth before. It was well-known that he was a tightwad.

Perry's wore his frugality like a badge of honor. We called him Ebenezer because he carried his money in an old-fashioned leather coin purse, the kind with a clasp closure. When it came to splitting a check at a pizza place or a diner, more times than not, Perry came up short on cash. He had a buck when his share should have been three. That was Perry, but as much as we made fun of him being cheap—no one actually complained it was all in good fun.

Norm took over at the wheel and was at the controls our first time docking the Richardson. *Captain Frank's* pier, crowded that day due to a baseball game, didn't have an open spot large enough for us. However, as we approached, a big cruiser vacated the end slip, and we slid right in to replace him. I jumped off the bow with a line, Kris did the same from the stern.

After lunch at the snack bar, we sat admiring the lines of our new boat, It was truly a classic. It had a forward cabin and an aft private stateroom. Between them was a large central salon with an enclosed helm. There was three private areas on the boat and that would give us all some privacy if desired. Built with luxury in mind, the double-planked mahogany hull was built to last. We saw a bright future for the Richardson.

On the trip home, Kris took the controls. We were curious about our fuel consumption rate; Norm and I guessed eight gallons per hour; Kris guessed ten.

Anxious to put a firm number on it, we turned into the Cleveland Yacht Club where we tied up at the fuel dock. According to our instruments, running time on the engines since fueling last night, had been three hours and thirty-five minutes. We'd taken on enough gas to bring us to the previous mark on the tank's sight-glass. As we read the numbers on the gas pump, the surprised look on my partner's' faces matched my own.

"Holy shit, we burned forty-nine gallons of gas in three and a half hours! That's forteen gallons per hour!" I said.

This revelation was of notable concern to us. I theorized that twelve knots might be a poor choice for a cruise speed. I'd have a look at the manual, and paperwork, that came with the boat. Our hull had been designed with an optimal cruising speed, we needed to know what it is.

I was at the wheel when we rounded the seawall into Gordon Park, blasting the air-horns to signaling our arrival, Hank and Ivan, were double-timing it to our pier. All our marina friends got the nickel-tour of the new boat.

That evening, we held an impromptu boat-warming party and headed to Fagin's in the Flats. We all had dates, so with Perry, Bob, and company, there were ten of us onboard. After dinner, we retreated to the boat's salon to continue the party. Around eleven, Fagin's manager came over and politely asked us to leave. Since we were drinking our own booze, we couldn't occupy half of their dock space on a Saturday night. It was understandable.

On the way back to the marina Perry's drunk new girlfriend fired our emergency flare pistol into the air. A huge orange glowing ball hung 500 feet above us for fifteen long-seconds. She intended it to be funny, but it was a serious offence that could cause us big problems.

We were drunk and stoned and the last thing we needed, was to be boarded by the Coast Guard. Radio chatter on channel sixteen tried to identify the source of the distress signal. Thankfully, no one saw where it originated.

* * *

After hearing about Larry bumping the old boat into the cruiser behind him, I walked over to have a look.

I couldn't see any stern damage on the old boat. The bow of the cruiser behind it, had some damage, but it looked old. What I *did* see was a ten-foot long scratch on the starboard side of the old *Day Tripper*. It looked to me like Larry scraped it against the pier support post, probably cutting too soon on his turn. The traces of white hull paint on the pier post-top confirmed my suspicion.

Later, Larry would tell me both incidents occurred the same day when his fishing buddy was too drunk to help him dock the boat.

* * *

Friday after work, a light drizzle fell as I picked up Mollie and we drove to Gordon Park. Monday was Labor Day, but since it rained continuously throughout the past week, we hadn't made holiday plans. However, last night's marine forecast called for high pressure and clear skies. With that in mind, I called the guys and we planned a three-day party.

Like Mollie and I, Kris, Norm, Bob, Perry, and their girlfriends, converged on the marina. Ten more friends would soon arrive, and Hank, his buddy Warren, and Ivan joined our weekend party. Warren, said he'd bring his ski-boat by tomorrow and everyone was welcome to join him. Since we all liked water skiing, we looked forward to a fun day. Now, all the party lacked was music.

Bob tuned his big short-wave radio to, CKLW, the 50,000-watt powerhouse AM rock station from Windsor, Ontario. On Friday evenings, they played full albums from dusk till dawn. That night, the station featured a new British band, Led Zeppelin. An odd name, but their music had a distinct, interesting sound. With the weather's cooperation, we had the makings of a fun holiday weekend.

Saturday morning brought the expected sunshine and calm air. While most of last night's guests still slept, I untied the dock-lines and backed the Richardson out of the slip. Per the plan, I headed over to *Captain Frank's* for brunch. On the way there, I ran the boat at full hull speed for the first time. The Richardson's thirty-eight-foot, full-displacement hull accelerated to almost twenty knots, leaving a huge wake in its trail. Below deck, the engines ran smooth and strong.

Warren said with obvious excitement, "You could ski behind this boat! I want to jump that wake!"

I told him I doubted a boat this size could pull up a skier. You had to consider the extra drag just to get him up.

The East 9th Street Pier, the home of Captain Frank's, was crowded that day; the White Sox were in town and the restaurant hosted their popular Saturday seafood brunch. Some of us went for it; the others headed around back to the snack-bar. I couldn't pass on bagels, lox, smoked fish and a Bloody Mary. After brunch, we dropped off Warren and Hank at Gordon Park and continued east to our *secluded* beach. Warren would join us there in a few hours.

The beach, with no easy land approach, was deserted as usual, but it was nearly covered with driftwood. We piled the wood into a tall stack, this will make a great fire.

Later that afternoon, Warren pulled up to the beach. By dusk, everyone who wanted to ski had done so. Before he left, Warren and I again discussed whether the Richardson could pull a skier, so before he left he handed me a canvas bag containing a pair of skis and a tow rope. I told him I'd try to settle our debate on the way home tomorrow.

It was a hot night and all of us opted to sleep on the beach instead of aboard the Richardson. The bonfire's flames were almost as high as the cliff above us. It didn't take long to realize we should have not have lit all the driftwood at the same time.

The lake, as flat as undisturbed bathwater, gave the illusion of the Richardson suspended in air. The hull eerily reflecting the fire's orange glow. Above us, a gibbous moon cast distinct hard shadows creating an image as clear today as it was fifty-years ago.

The next day the good weather held out. We played on the beach all day, sunbathing, swimming, and fishing. By late afternoon, we considered another night on the beach, but being nearly out of food and booze stifled that plan. We'd go back to the marina, restock and continue the party dockside.

That night our friend and pot dealer, Stash, arrived at Gordon Park with a couple of friends and the party continued strong. By dawn, the last of our guests departed. Still aboard were Mollie and I, Kris and Susan. We all slept until late that afternoon, then headed to our fishing spot north of the east breakwall light. After landing enough yellow perch for dinner, we were ready to head in. Kris said, "Do you want to try the water ski experiment now?"

"No time like the present," I said, grabbing the skis and heading aft.

The girls watched from the rear deck as I jumped in and readied myself. Kris was at the controls as I gave a thumbs-up gesture. Mollie relayed my signal to Kris and off we went. The slower takeoff speed put a lot of strain on my arms and legs but I held on tight. Then, I was up! Skiing side to side within the wake to maintain enough speed to stay up, Warren was right.

Then I sank into the water as a white puff of smoke drifted behind the boat. *That can't be good*, I thought. Just then, the rope tightened as the girls pulled me toward the transom. Neither engine was running.

In the salon, the deck hatches were open; Kris knelt by the port engine. There was nothing to see, so we'll figure it out back at the dock. When he tried the port starter button the engine only backfired. I closed the engine hatches and Kris started the starboard engine. *Maybe it's an ignition issue.*

With the port engine down, the drag from its non-working propeller caused the boat to pull hard to the left requiring significant rudder compensation just to keep us on course. Our forward speed slowed to below four-knots.

A half a mile out from Gordon Park, we could see the old *Day Tripper* leaving the marina heading west west. I'd never before seen it from this distant perspective. I grabbed my binoculars and looked again.

It sure is a good-looking boat, I thought. With our current engine situation looming on my mind, seeing the *Day Tripper* brought on doubts. *Maybe we acted too fast with our decision to replace it.*

* * *

Back at the dock, a quick look-see showed no compression in cylinder two of the port engine. Since Labor Day was the next day, we'd finish our three-days of partying at the dock. We still had the Weber along with food and drinks. The engine problem could wait until next weekend. Bob offered to lend a hand.

The following weekend, after removing the cylinder head we discovered that the engine had a broken connecting rod. The correct solution would have been to rebuild both engines. We opted for a cheaper resolution—replace only the connecting rod, and hope for the best.

A week later, after gathering all the parts and equipment, we began a marathon repair session. We'd work straight through until the job was finished.

Ivan loaned us a long 6x6 wood beam that we placed through both of the salon's side doors. The beam supported the winch used to raise the engine off its motor mounts. With the engine high enough to get under the crankshaft, Bob removed the broken connecting rod along with the piston. Luckily, the engine block had no apparent damage.

Hours later, with the new parts installed, we began re-assembling the engine. Bob's brother, Danny, came by later in the day to help with the finishing-up work under the raised engine block. He connected the oil pump pickup line, attached the oil pan, and re-bolted the engine to its mounts. Danny adding two and a half gallons of motor oil completed the job.

Norm pressed the starter button and the engine fired up running smooth and steady after a minute. We were dirty, tired, and hungry, but, the job went without a major hitch. By midnight, we were done. We picked up two pizzas and a twelve-pack. It had been a long, hard, day.

At around 6AM, Junior slapped hard on our hull getting our attention. He called out, "Lenny, Lenny!

We got a big problem!"

This was not a good way to start the day.

"What's up?" I said, seeing a scowling Junior on the pier.

Pointing to the water, he said, "Look at this shit—there's oil everywhere."

He was right, the marina surface looked like an oil slick. Most of the boats berthed on the first two piers had an oil ring surrounding their hulls. We had neglected to turn off our automatic pumps and the engine oil that mistakenly spilled into our bilge during repairs, got pumped into the marina.

Using dish soap on a sponge, while we worked from the pier and a rowboat, the cleanup took us all day. It was reminiscent of the aftermath of last year's infamous fish-scale explosion

CHAPTER 23:
THE END OF THE END

A couple of late summer thunderstorms came through the area, rain fell throughout the week. On Friday, the girls were aboard and we decided to head up to *Captain Frank's*. This would be the first time out for the Richardson since the engine repair.

I maintained a lower speed inside the marina and its outer basin. Upon reaching the lake, I pushed forward on the throttles bringing the engines to 1,200 rpm. Scanning the gauges, everything looked good.

The light rain didn't bother us inside the cabin. Unlike the *Day Tripper*, we could operate comfortably in inclement weather. Wiper blades cleared our forward view as Norm took over at the wheel.

Mollie and I moved to the big leather couch where Kris talked about installing an AM/FM stereo with a built-in 8-track tape player.

About then, we felt the engines coming out of sync creating a distinct vibration pattern. Wondering what was going on, Kris and I both looked toward Norm.

"That wasn't me! Something's going on," he said.

I sprang to the instrument panel and scanned the gauges. The port engine oil pressure was at zero!

Before I could close the throttle, a loud ominous squeal came from below deck as the port engine shook the boat, then shut down all by itself.

Kris opened the floor-hatch and the pungent smell of burnt oil filled the cabin. He grabbed a flashlight and stepped into the engine compartment. A few seconds later he called out, "No nooooo! Shit! Shit! Shit!

Standing up, he held the foot-long oil pump pickup line in his hand, it was sitting under the port engine. My heart sank as I realized the severity of the situation. There was no oil circulation. Danny had not attached the oil pick-up line!

Without it, the engine couldn't draw oil from the sump during acceleration. The squeal and shudder was the final sound of a seizing engine.

No one said a word as we turned the boat around. We were limping home again on our starboard engine. This was truly a Déjà vu moment. Two weeks earlier the same engine quit on us. Back then, there was hope that the problem was repairable. This time that same optimism was not present.

I couldn't fathom how we would even replace an engine in a boat like this. I guessed the entire salon would have to be removed. *How the hell could we do that?* This was beyond our abilities or resources.

Back in the marina, after securing the boat in its slip, everyone headed to our apartment. We hoped drinks and pizza would help ease our pain.

On the drive home, I thought about something Junior recently told me.

When I complained about the money we'd just spent fixing the boat, he said. "Haven't you heard—a boat is a hole in the water, that you fill with money."

We chuckled and I said, "Here's another one Junior—B O A T is an acronym, it stands for—Bust Out Another Thousand."

Somehow, it all seemed funnier last week.

* * *

Making inquiries, I discovered that both engines would have to be rebuilt or replaced. The project could probably be completed over the winter storage season. We were quoted five to seven thousand dollars, maybe (probably) more.

We decided to put the Richardson up for sale. It was our only option. The next morning I posted an ad in the Cleveland Plain Dealer classified section,

I listed the Richardson for $4,000. Over the next week four prospective buyers looked at the boat. Two of them went for a ride, and one offered us $2,800.

Negotiations brought us to $3,500 and with a simple handshake we were former yachtsmen.

* * *

Four months later, Norm called me at work to say he thought he saw the *Day Tripper* loaded on the back of a flatbed trailer. On his way to work, he passed Gordon Park and happened to look towards the big municipal parking lot. Although on the freeway and catching only a quick glimpse, he was almost sure he saw the old boat. We made plans to meet there at lunchtime.

Norm was right. The *Day Tripper* lay partially crumbled by its own weight atop a flatbed tractor-trailer rig.

Covered with snow and held down tight by straps and chains, there was no doubt the scrap yard would be its next destination. It was sad to see the boat in such an undignified state when it had brought so much joy into our lives.

It felt like I was paying my last respects to an old friend. Norm and I were somewhat consoled knowing that for the last two years we were able to extend its life and function. My eyes teared-up a little on the drive back to work. The next morning, Norm called to say the truck with the boat was gone.

Although I tried to contact Larry to find out what happened, I was unable to reach him. Hank couldn't find him either. Junior told me the boat was still in the water when he closed in early December.

That spring Junior called to say he'd found out that the *Day Tripper* had floated into the Intercity Yacht Club's docks. He believed they had it removed.

I thanked him for the new information.

* * *

The *Day Tripper*, built in 1941 as a lifeboat, ended up repurposed in the sixties into one hell of a pleasure craft.

That boat introduced us to new people, places, experiences, and adventures. Owning it reshaped our lives forever. By any standard, the *Day Tripper* served above and beyond anyone's expectations.

Today, nearly half a century later, I can summarize my recollection of the whole experience into one memory, one vision. I close my eyes, draw in a deep breath, let it out slowly—and in my mind's eye, I see:

It's just before sunset. Kris and Norm stand on the forward deck as we come around the windward side of South Bass Island. The beauty of Put-in-Bay's picturesque harbor unfolds before us. The sun setting in a tangerine sky, casts long shadows over hundreds of colorful boats anchored around the bay.

As church bells ring in the distance, a warm offshore breeze carries the scent of jasmine. Welcomed by the cries of hungry gulls, we motor into the harbor.

The End

EPILOGUE

Mollie and I married in the winter of 1970. A year later Kris also wed. He met a wonderful girl named Joan, and she came with a two-year-old son. Kris had an instant family. It suited him well, he's a great father.

In the mid-seventies, Norm was the last of our three to marry. He was also the first to leave Cleveland. When his new father-in-law retired to Phoenix and opened a high-end men's shoe store, Norm was offered a management position. He couldn't refuse the opportunity.

Mollie and Joan became close friends and the four of us spent most of our leisure time together. Kris bought a 25-foot cabin cruiser, *The Euphoria*. He kept it at Mentor Lagoons near his home. Over the years, we had many fun times on and around that boat.

Kris became a successful business owner. I always felt that that the schmoozing he developed to win over girls as a teenager, evolved into a successful business technique. He strived for success and achieved it. Kris and Joan now live in Estero, Florida.

Mollie and I split up after nine years. It didn't work out for us but, we parted as friends. The last I'd heard she lived in Miami with a guy named John who owned a BBQ restaurant..

In '76, Bob's entire family picked up and moved to Florida in one swoop. His father opened a used Rolls Royce/Bentley dealership and Bob served as his first mechanic, auto-body repairman, and painter. They did quite well for themselves.

I never saw Junior again, although I did run into Della years later on a downtown street. She told me the City wouldn't be renewing their fifteen-year lease at Gordon Park. They'd be making other plans for the future.

Years later, I heard Hank had died. He was quite the character. I never saw him without his blue crested-pocket blazer and his signature white captain's cap. His boat rarely left its slip, but there were plenty of good times aboard the aptly named, *Hanky Panky*.

Kris had heard that Ivan and his family moved to Florida and he would to try and track him down. Ivan, a mechanical genius, could do anything. Kris never found him.

I lost contact with Perry in the late eighties. He had become reclusive after receiving a large inheritance. Perry, the perfectionist, could never be rushed. When he did something, you could be sure it was done right.

Kris, Norm, and I see each other every year or so. We talk, text, and email all of the time. From the seventh grade forward, we have always been the best of friends. I'm sure that bond will continue to the end.

Bob became ill and passed away in 2016. Kris and I visited him at his Pompano Beach home a short time before his death. We knew it would be the last time we'd see each other. It was so hard to say goodbye. Bob and I had been friends since we were five.

By 1980, newly divorced and fed up with snow, slush, and bad weather, I made plans to move to Florida. After selling everything but a carload of possessions, I was days away from heading south to a new life in Ft. Lauderdale. At least, that was my plan until a 5 AM phone call changed my life.

When the phone rings before dawn, it's seldom good news, and this was no exception. My mother, in a self-controlled voice, told me she had terminal lung cancer. She was 66 and could expect to live just one more year.

My father had passed away six years earlier. After that, my mother met a nice guy, remarried and they retired in San Diego.

Hearing her news changed my plans and direction. I went west to be with my mother and help her through whatever time she had left. After that, I'd move to Florida, where I had planned to go, in the first place.

However, as I settled into life on the west coast, I realized that I liked it here. I had made new friends, had a good job in the graphic arts field, bought a motorcycle and a '65 Mustang. I had become comfortable with the California lifestyle.

– Len Berman

Gordon Park Sept. 1968

The Day Tripper